JOURNEYS AND DESTINATIONS

▼

A Language Arts Unit for High-Ability Learners

Grades 2–3

The College of William and Mary
School of Education
Center for Gifted Education
Williamsburg, VA 23187-8795

JOURNEYS AND DESTINATIONS

A Language Arts Unit for High-Ability Learners

Grades 2–3

The College of William and Mary
School of Education
Center for Gifted Education
Williamsburg, VA 23187-8795

Center for Gifted Education Staff:
Project Director: Dr. Joyce VanTassel-Baska

Project Manager: Dana T. Johnson

Project Consultants: Linda Neal Boyce, Chwee Quek, Claire Hughes, Catherine A. Little

Teacher Developer:
Carol Cawley

Funded by the Jacob K. Javits Program, United States Department of Education,
under a subcontract from the Washington-Saratoga-Warren-Hamilton-Essex BOCES,
Saratoga Springs, New York.

KENDALL/HUNT PUBLISHING COMPANY
4050 Westmark Drive   Dubuque, Iowa 52002

Contents

SECTION I: UNIT INTRODUCTION AND CURRICULUM FRAMEWORK   1

SECTION II: LESSON PLANS   7

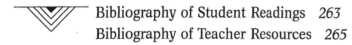

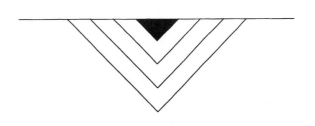

SECTION

I

UNIT INTRODUCTION AND CURRICULUM FRAMEWORK

This section provides the rationale for the unit and the core goals and student outcomes that frame its lessons. It also lists student reading selections, both core works and those used in extension assignments.

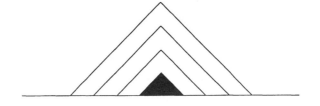

▼ Introduction to the Unit

The guiding theme of this unit is the recognition that change affects people and their relationships as well as the world around them. The literature selections of the unit illustrate this theme for students. Activities of the unit engage students in discussion and writing about what they have read, and in independent and group learning opportunities that promote skill development in vocabulary, persuasive writing, literary analysis, oral communication, and thinking. Discussion emphasizes the search for meaning in literature. Students also engage in research on the role of memory in their lives and the role of technology in preserving memories.

▼ Rationale and Purpose

A language arts curriculum should expose high ability students to exemplary works of literature that challenge their critical reasoning and nurture their search for meaning in an ongoing quest to understand themselves and those within their world. This unit provides such a quest. Moreover, it provides a myriad array of opportunities for student learning in the core language arts strands of reading, writing, oral communication, and language study.

▼ Goals and Outcomes

Content Goals and Outcomes

GOAL #1: To develop analytical and interpretive skills in literature.

Students will be able to . . .

    A. Describe what a selected literary passage means.

    B. Cite similarities and differences in meaning among selected works of literature.

    C. Make inferences based on information in given passages.

    D. Create a title for a reading selection and provide a rationale to justify it.

GOAL #2: To develop persuasive writing skills.

Students will be able to . . .

    A. Develop a written persuasive paragraph (thesis statement, supporting reasons, and conclusion), given a topic.

    B. Complete various pieces of writing using a three-phase revision process based on peer review, teacher feedback, and self-evaluation.

GOAL #3: To develop linguistic competency.

Students will be able to . . .

    A. Develop vocabulary power commensurate with reading.

    B. Apply standard English usage in written and oral contexts.

    C. Evaluate effective use of words, sentences, and paragraphs in context.

GOAL #4: To develop listening/oral communication skills.

Students will be able to . . .

    A. Organize oral presentations.

    B. Evaluate an oral presentation, given a rubric of specific criteria.

Process Goal and Outcomes

GOAL #5: To develop reasoning skills in the language arts.

Students will be able to . . .

    A. Apply aspects of the Paul reasoning model through specific examples.

    B. State a purpose for all modes of communication, their own as well as others.

    C. Define a problem, given ill-structured, complex, or technical information.

    D. Formulate multiple perspectives (at least two) on a given issue.

    E. Apply linguistic and literary concepts appropriately.

    F. Provide evidence and data to support a claim, issue, or thesis statement.

    G. Make inferences, based on evidence.

Concept Goal and Outcomes

GOAL #6: To understand the concept of change in the language arts.*

Students will be able to . . .

    A. Understand that change is pervasive.

    B. Illustrate the variability of change based on time.

    C. Categorize types of change, given several examples.

    D. Interpret change as positive or negative in selected works.

    E. Identify elements of change in a piece of literature.

    F. Analyze social and individual change in a given piece of literature.

*See the Appendix for a detailed discussion of the concept of change.

▼ Student Readings

Novels/Books

The Green Book	Jill Paton Walsh	(Lessons 4, 7, 8, 9, 10)
Mission to Deep Space: Voyagers' Journey of Discovery	William E. Burrows	(Lesson 7)
Free Fall	David Wiesner	(Lesson 13)
Bringing the Rain to Kapiti Plain	Verna Aardema	(Lesson 17)
Sachiko Means Happiness	Kimiko Sakai	(Lesson 19)
Emma's Dragon Hunt	Catherine Stock	(Lesson 19)

Short Stories

"The Wolf and the Lion"	*Aesop for Children*	(Lessons 1, 4)
"Shells"	Cynthia Rylant	(Lessons 3, 4)
"The Ugly Duckling"	Hans Christian Andersen	(Lessons 15, 16)
"The Green Man"	Gail E. Haley	(Lesson 21)
"The Miser"	*Aesop for Children*	(Lesson 24)
Iroquois Stories (audio tapes)	Joseph Bruchac	(Learning Center)

Poems

"poem for rodney"	Nikki Giovanni	(Lesson 11)
"Perfection"	Felice Holman	(Lesson 11)
"Poem"	Langston Hughes	(Lesson 11)

Additional Books Referenced in Homework Assignments

Hailstones and Halibut Bones	Mary O'Neill	(Lesson 12)
Rain Player	David Wisniewski	(Lesson 17)

Resources for Optional Extensions

Lesson Extensions:

All I See	Cynthia Rylant	(Lessons 3, 4)
An Angel for Solomon Singer	Cynthia Rylant	(Lessons 3, 4)

SECTION

II

LESSON PLANS

The pages which follow provide some introductory information about the unit lessons, including a discussion of the alignment of lessons with unit goals, lists of key vocabulary words, and a letter to send home to parents about the unit. The unit lesson plans themselves appear after the parent letter.

▼ Alignment of Lessons with Unit Goals

The table below demonstrates which lessons contain activities specifically addressing each of the overall unit goals.

GOAL	LESSONS
Goal 1: Literary analysis and interpretation	1, 3, 7, 8, 9, 10, 11, 15, 17, 19, 21, 22, 23, 24
Goal 2: Persuasive writing	1, 5, 6, 8, 9, 11, 12, 13, 15, 18, 19, 21, 22, 23, 24
Goal 3: Linguistic competency	4, 7, 8, 9, 15, 17, 19, 21
Goal 4: Oral communication	14, 20, 22
Goal 5: Reasoning	6, 10, 16
Goal 6: Concept of change	2, 11, 13, 16, 23, 24

Other emphases are also specifically addressed, as indicated in the following table:

EMPHASIS	LESSONS
Interdisciplinary Connections	4, 7, 10, 13, 16, 17, 19
Student Research	10, 18, 22

▼ Unit Vocabulary List

The list of words below contains suggested words for vocabulary study from each literature selection in the unit. The teaching model employed for vocabulary study is introduced in Lesson 4 and used throughout the unit; it is also described under "Teaching Models" in Section III.

from "The Wolf and the Lion":
evil
excuse
inconvenience
injure
lair
shepherd

from "Shells":
condominium
dramatic
dully
fiercely
founding father
inherit
linoleum
phenomenon
prejudiced
Presbyterian
stupor

from *The Green Book*:
allocated
biorhythms
flagons
fodder
hexagon
hostile
malfunction
perishable
rapt
rations

relevant
rivulet
runnel
scudding
treacle
wistfully

from "The Ugly Duckling":
admonished
aristocratic
mocked
persecuted
probation
scoundrel

from *Bringing the Rain to Kapiti Plain*:
migrated
pasture
stork

from *Sachiko Means Happiness*:
crossly
impatiently
reassure
reflected
timidly

from *The Green Man*:
arrogant
defiant
glean
tether

▼ Glossary of Literary Terms

The following list contains a selection of literary terms which may be useful for students to understand in the discussion of literature in the unit.

Character: a person portrayed in an artistic piece, such as a drama or novel

Climax: the turning point in a plot or dramatic action; a moment of great or culminating intensity in a narrative or drama, especially at the conclusion of a crisis

Denouement: the final resolution or clarification of a dramatic or narrative plot; the events following the climax of a drama or novel in which such a resolution or clarification takes place

Motivation: an inducement or incentive to action; in a story, the psychological or social factors that drive character action

Plot: the plan of events or main story in a narrative or drama

Setting: the time, place, and circumstances in which a narrative, drama, or film takes place

Theme: an implicit or recurrent idea; a motif; a central idea that permeates a poem, short story, or novel

Dear Parents:

Your child is engaged in a special language arts unit called *Journeys and Destinations*. It is designed specifically to meet the needs of high ability students. The goals of the unit are as follows:

▼ To develop analytical and interpretive skills in literature.

▼ To develop persuasive writing skills.

▼ To develop linguistic competency.

▼ To develop listening/oral communication skills.

▼ To develop reasoning skills.

▼ To understand the concept of change.

A wide variety of literature will provide the context for our exploration of change. The literature will stimulate discussion, writing, listening, vocabulary study, and research activities. In class, we will read and discuss short pieces of literature—poems, short stories, fables, speeches, and essays. Everyone will keep a response journal to clarify thinking and to help prepare for written and oral assignments. As we read the literature, we will respond to it and think critically about it by analyzing ideas, vocabulary, and structure. Specifically, we will look for insight into the concept of change.

This unit includes the following activities which will require some work outside of class and may need your support at home:

▼ Independent reading that includes selected stories and books

▼ Written homework assignments

▼ A research project on ways to preserve memories

▼ An in-class project requiring two photos of your child at different ages

Independent work will be discussed in class, and further information will be sent home as assignments are given. There will be opportunities for students to work with the teacher and classmates on each project as the unit progresses. The time frame for these projects is summarized in the schedule on the following page.

Student progress in the unit will be assessed in several ways. First, a pre-test will assess skill level in the language arts areas of literature and writing. Secondly, a writing portfolio will document progress in writing. We will assess a number of writing pieces through three perspectives: self, peer, and teacher. I also welcome comments and feedback from parents on how the unit is progressing.

LESSON NUMBER AND DATE ASSIGNED		DESCRIPTION OF ASSIGNMENT	LESSON NUMBER AND DUE DATE	
Lesson 8 (date:	)	Writing Assignment 1 "Special Objects"	a. Lesson 9 (revising) (date:	)
			b. Lesson 10 (editing) (date:	)
Lesson 10 (date:	)	Research on "memories"	Lesson 22 (date:	)
Lesson 11 (date:	)	Writing Assignment 2 "Writing about Change"	a. Lesson 12 (revising) (date:	)
			b. Lesson 13 (editing) (date:	)
Lesson 18 (date:	)	Writing Assignment 3 "Ways to Preserve Memories"	Lesson 22 Written report and oral presentation (date:	)

Good curriculum and instructional practice should involve parents as well as teachers. The following ideas may be useful as your child experiences the unit:

1. Read the stories and books your child is reading and discuss the key ideas.

2. Hold a family debate on one of the issues discussed in the unit.

3. Play word games such as Scrabble® or Boggle® with the family to enhance vocabulary and language usage.

4. Encourage your child to write every day in a diary or log.

5. Try to set up a letter-writing arrangement with someone from another country or another part of the United States in order to encourage writing on a regular basis, either through regular or electronic mail.

6. When viewing film or television together, discuss the ideas presented with your child, and encourage close attention to how ideas are handled in the media.

Thank you in advance for your interest in your child's curriculum. Please do not hesitate to contact me for further information as the unit progresses.

Sincerely,

LESSON

1

Introduction and Pre-Assessment

CURRICULUM ALIGNMENT CODE

GOAL 1	GOAL 2	GOAL 3	GOAL 4	GOAL 5	GOAL 6
X	X			X	X

INSTRUCTIONAL PURPOSE

▼ To develop reasoning and interpretive skills in literature by discussing the fable "The Wolf and the Lion."

▼ To administer the unit pre-assessments in literature and writing.

MATERIALS USED

1. "The Wolf and the Lion"

2. Pre-Assessment for Literature (Handout 1A)

3. Literature Interpretation Scoring Rubric for Pre- and Post-Assessments

4. Pre-Assessment for Writing (Handout 1B)

5. Persuasive Writing Scoring Rubric for Pre- and Post-Assessments

ACTIVITIES

1. Have students read the story "The Wolf and the Lion" and take the **Pre-Assessment for Literature** (Handout 1A).

2. Have students keep their papers and the story to discuss the pre-assessment questions. Guide the discussion further with additional questions such as the following:

   ▼ *What is meant by the words, "as Wolf was too far away to be taught a lesson without too much inconvenience"?*

   ▼ *What do you think Wolf might have answered to Lion's question?*

   ▼ *What was the Lion's purpose in taking the Lamb from the Wolf?*

15

3. Have students discuss which aspects of the pre-assessment they found difficult, and explain that throughout the unit they will learn more about reading literature and thinking about challenging questions such as those on the pre-assessment.

4. Collect the **Pre-Assessment for Literature**.

5. Distribute the **Pre-Assessment for Writing**. Have students complete the pre-assessment, then discuss the pre-assessment writing question. After the discussion, collect the papers.

NOTES TO TEACHER

1. *Please send home the letter to parents (see p. 13) with each student who is engaged in the unit. Remember to sign the letter and to fill in tentative dates for assignment deadlines.*

2. *The pre-assessments in literature and persuasive writing serve multiple purposes. Performance on the pre-assessment should establish a baseline against which performance on the post-assessment may be compared. In addition, teachers may use information obtained from the pre-assessments to aid instructional planning as strengths and weaknesses of students become apparent. Rubrics are provided for the scoring of the pre- and post-assessments, followed by sample student responses with their scores.*

Pre-Assessment for Literature
(Handout 1A)

NAME: _____ DATE: _____

Please read the passage and answer the questions.

1. State an important idea of the story in a sentence or two.

2. Use your own words to describe what you think the author means by the words, "What is evil won is evil lost."

3. What does the story tell us about the idea of change? Support what you say with details from the story.

4. Create a title for this story. Give two reasons from the story for your new title.

17

Literature Interpretation Scoring Rubric for Pre- and Post-Assessments

1. **State an important idea of the reading in a sentence or two.**

Score	Description of Response
1	limited, vague, inaccurate, confusing, only quotes from reading
2	simplistic, literal statement; uses only part of main idea; creates title rather than main idea
3	insightful, addresses theme

2. **Use your own words to describe what you think the author means by . . .**

Score	Description of Response
1	limited, vague, inaccurate; rewording only
2	accurate but literal response
3	insightful, interpretive response

3. **What does the story tell us about the idea of change? Support what you say with details from the story.**

Score	Description of Response
1	limited, vague, inaccurate; only quotes from story
2	valid generalization without support **or** well-supported example
3	valid generalization about change is made and well supported

4. **Create a title for this story. Give two reasons from the story for your new title.**

Score	Description of Response
1	limited, vague, or title given without reasons
2	appropriate but literal response; at least one reason given
3	insightful, meaningful title given with support

Sample Student Responses
Pre-Assessment for Literature

1. **State an important idea of the reading in a sentence or two.**

   SAMPLE 1-POINT RESPONSES:

   - *An important idea of this story is: What is evil won is evil lost.*
   - *The wolf stole the lamb.*

   SAMPLE 2-POINT RESPONSE:

   - *I think the main idea of the story is that no one should ever steal.*

   SAMPLE 3-POINT RESPONSES:

   - *If you do something bad something bad will happen to you.*
   - *Other people will do bad things to you if you do bad things to them.*

2. **Use your own words to describe what you think the author means by . . .**

   SAMPLE 1-POINT RESPONSES:

   - *What evil won it loses.*
   - *He means that the lamb is stolen but now it is lost.*

   SAMPLE 2-POINT RESPONSES:

   - *Never take things from other people or other people will take yours.*
   - *If you are not nice and you get something you could lose it.*

   SAMPLE 3-POINT RESPONSE:

   - *It means if you are evil and win, you have really lost in the long run.*

3. **What does the story tell us about the idea of change? Support with details.**

   SAMPLE 1-POINT RESPONSE:

   - *His plans were very much changed when he met the lion.*

   SAMPLE 2-POINT RESPONSES:

   - *When the Wolf thought he got the Lamb the Lion came and took it away. It sounded like the Wolf was happy but as soon as the Lion came along the Wolf's happiness changed.*
   - *I think the story tells us about things that you plan don't always turn out to be the way you think.*

SAMPLE 3-POINT RESPONSE:

- *Changes can be good and bad. First the Wolf had the Lamb and then the Lion had it. That was a good change for the Lion and a bad change for the Wolf.*

4. **Create a title for this story. Give two reasons from the story for your new title.**

SAMPLE 1-POINT RESPONSES:

- *The Lamb, the Lion, and the Wolf. Because the story involves a lamb, a lion, and a wolf.*
- *I would call it Stealing.*

SAMPLE 2-POINT RESPONSES:

- *Two Evil Animals. I would call it this because the lion and the wolf did an evil thing.*
- *The Wolf, the Lion, and the Stolen Lunch. Because the characters were the wolf and the lion. Because the lamb was stolen by the wolf.*

SAMPLE 3-POINT RESPONSE:

- *Whose Lamb is it? They are having a fight about whose it really is.*

Pre-Assessment for Writing

(Handout 1B)

NAME: _____ DATE: _____

Directions: Write a paragraph to answer the question below. State your opinion, include three reasons for your opinion, and write a conclusion to your paragraph.

Do you think the story, "The Wolf and the Lion," should be required reading for all students in your grade?

Persuasive Writing Scoring Rubric for Pre- and Post-Assessments

Claim or Opinion

Score	Description of Response
0	No clear position exists on the writer's assertion, preference, or view, and context does not help clarify it.
2	Yes/no alone or writer's position is poorly formulated, but reader is reasonably sure what the paper is about because of context.
4	A basic topic sentence exists, and the reader is reasonably sure what the paper is about based on the strength of the topic sentence alone.
6	A very clear, concise position is given as a topic sentence, and the reader is very certain what the paper is about. Must include details such as grade level, title of the reading, or reference to "the story," etc.

Data or Supporting Points

Score	Description of Response
0	No data are offered that are relevant to the claim.
2	Scant data (one or two pieces) are offered, but what data exist are relevant to the claim.
4	At least three pieces of data are offered. They are relevant but not necessarily convincing or complete.
6	At least three pieces of accurate and convincing data are offered.

Warrant or Elaboration on Data

Score	Description of Response
0	No warrant or elaboration is offered.
2	An attempt is made to elaborate at least one element of the data.
4	More than one piece of data is explained, but the explanation is weak and lacks thoroughness, **or** one piece of data is well elaborated.
6	The writer explains more than one piece of data in such a way that it is clear how they support the argument. At least one piece of data is convincingly and completely elaborated.

(Adapted from N. Burkhalter, 1995)

Conclusion

Score	Description of Response
0	No conclusion/closing sentence is provided.
2	A conclusion/closing sentence is provided.

Sample Student Responses
Pre-Assessment for Writing

Sample 1

No, I don't think so because: some students are above or below the reading levels. I think that some would say, "This is too easy," others would say, "This is too hard!"

Score: Claim = 2   Total Score = 6
        Data = 2
        Warrant = 2
        Conclusion = 0

Sample 2

Yes, I think it should be required reading for students in my grade. I think that because it is confusing and is a challenge to figure out what "what is evil won is evil lost" means.

Score: Claim = 4   Total Score = 8
        Data = 2
        Warrant = 2
        Conclusion = 0

Sample 3

Yes, I think the story "The Wolf and the Lion" should be required reading for all the students. Why? It's a great story with a very interesting topic. They could also learn from the story. Also they could get lots of interesting questions. That is why I think 3rd grade students should read "The Wolf and the Lion."

Score: Claim = 6   Total Score = 12
        Data = 4
        Warrant = 2
        Conclusion = 2

Sample 4

No, I don't think all third graders should read this book. First of all because it is kind of short and most third graders like longer books. Also because I don't think it is very interesting and does not include a lot of detail. Most of all because it's like a little kids book and most third graders don't like the topic of talking animals.

Score: Claim = 6   Total Score = 14
        Data = 4
        Warrant = 4
        Conclusion = 0

LESSON

2

The Concept of Change

CURRICULUM ALIGNMENT CODE

GOAL 1	GOAL 2	GOAL 3	GOAL 4	GOAL 5	GOAL 6
				X	X

INSTRUCTIONAL PURPOSE

▼ To introduce the concept of change.

MATERIALS USED

1. Change Model (Handout 2A)
2. Large paper and markers

ACTIVITIES

1. Explain to students that the **concept of change** will be the basis of their journey into the literature in this unit. Divide students into groups of four or five and distribute large paper and markers to each groups. Use the following questions to guide an introductory discussion on change; groups may write or draw their responses on the large paper and then share ideas with the class.

Brainstorm ideas about change and write down all responses on the large paper.

▼ *What do you think of when you hear the word* **change**? *What kinds of things change? What is it about them that changes?*

Categorize the ideas that were written down, putting them into groups and titling each group.

▼ *How could you put your change ideas into groups? How are some of the changes alike?*

▼ *What could you call each group? Why?*

▼ *Could some of your changes belong to more than one group? Why? What are some different ways you might categorize your changes?*

▼ *What do your ideas tell you about changes in general? What are some of the **characteristics** of change?*

Brainstorm a list of things that do not change, and write them on another sheet of large paper.

▼ *What are some things that are always the same or that always happen the same way?*

▼ *Look at the list of things that change. While those things are changing, can you think of anything else that stays the same?*

▼ *What can you say about the ideas of things that do not change? How could you put them into groups?*

▼ *What could you call each group? Why?*

▼ *Think about these ideas and whether they show change: routines or habits, rules and regulations, table manners, laws, customs of cultures. Explain your answers. If they do show change, where would they fit into your categories of changes? If they do not, where would they fit into your categories of things that do not change?*

Make generalizations about change.

▼ *A **generalization** is something that is always or almost always true. Can you say something that is always or almost always true about change?*

▼ *Look at the categories of changes we found and see if they help you make generalizations about change. How are our examples alike?*

2. Share the following list and explain that it is the core set of generalizations that is used for this unit. Have students compare these to their set. Help them to align their generalizations with the set below. Discuss them, using the suggested questions as a guide.

▼ *Change is linked to time. (How is change linked to time? Why do different changes take different amounts of time to happen?)*

▼ *Change may be positive or negative. (Which of the changes we discussed would we call good changes? Which are bad changes? Are there any that could be good and bad? How? Does change always represent progress, or making things better?)*

▼ *Change may be perceived as orderly or random. (Can we predict change? What are some changes you know will happen and how they will happen, and what are some that are surprises?)*

▼ *Change is everywhere. (Does change happen all areas of our world? Where have you seen changes happening in the world around you?)*

▼ *Change may happen naturally or be caused by people. (What causes change? What are some changes that people can't do anything about? What are some changes that can't happen without people?)*

3. Discuss the following question regarding change: How do our ideas about change and its generalizations apply or not apply to the things below?

▼ *non-living things (e.g., a chair, a pair of scissors)*

▼ *traditions (e.g., special holidays, celebrations of birth, passage, and death)*

▼ *religious rituals (e.g., celebrations of Christmas or Hanukkah)*

▼ *universal truths (e.g., all living things die; all triangles have three sides)*

4. Have students work in their groups to complete the attached **Change Model** (Handout 2A) in groups of 4–5. (Note: It may be preferable to allow students to copy the model onto larger paper for this activity.) Encourage students to draw or write ideas which support each of the five generalizations about change. Provide time for groups to share their ideas with the class. Completed Change Models may be displayed in the classroom, and students should also be given copies to keep in their notebooks for reference throughout the unit.

5. Close by explaining that we will be looking at many aspects of change as we explore this unit, including changes in our own lives and the world around us as well as in the stories and poems we read. Encourage students to think about change and watch for changes around them which support the five generalizations.

NOTES TO TEACHER

1. *The concept development model employed in this lesson is explained in detail in the implementation section at the end of the unit. Stages of the model may be expanded as necessary for adequate development of student understanding.*

2. *Lessons throughout the unit will refer to the list of generalizations included in this lesson. These generalizations should be posted in the classroom, and students should keep their Change Models in their notebooks for reference throughout the unit. The generalizations developed by students should be aligned to this set and may also be posted and used for reference throughout the unit.*

HOMEWORK

Choose one of the generalizations about change. Write a paragraph explaining why it is true. Give at least three reasons or examples to support your main idea.

EXTENSION

Observe change around you by charting one of these over the course of one week:

▼ temperature change

▼ mood change in a family member

▼ lead news stories on p. 1 of your local newspaper

▼ the evening meal at your house

Change Model
(Handout 2A)

NAME: _____ DATE: _____

Develop a list of three–five examples for each of the following statements (generalizations) about change.

Change is linked to time:

Change is everywhere:

Change

Change may be positive:

. . . or negative:

Change may be perceived as orderly:

. . . or random:

Change may happen naturally:

or may be caused by people:

LESSON

3

Introduction to Literature Interpretation

CURRICULUM ALIGNMENT CODE

GOAL 1	GOAL 2	GOAL 3	GOAL 4	GOAL 5	GOAL 6
X	X			X	X

INSTRUCTIONAL PURPOSE

▼ To develop reasoning and interpretive skills in literature by discussing the story "Shells" by Cynthia Rylant.

▼ To develop an understanding of the concept of change.

MATERIALS USED

1. "Shells," by Cynthia Rylant*

2. Literature Web—Teacher Example

3. Literature Web—Primary Adaptation (Handout 3A)

4. Student Response Journals

5. Change Matrix (Handout 3B)

ACTIVITIES

1. Distribute copies of Cynthia Rylant's story "Shells" for students to read silently.

2. Introduce a **Literature Web** (Handout 3A). Show a blank copy of the web on the overhead and talk through each part with the class, using the questions below and the completed example to guide the discussion. Students may fill in individual copies of the Literature Web for their notebooks during discussion.

   a. **Key Words:** Think and look back over the story. What were some words or groups of words that you really liked or thought were really important? Why

*Rylant, C. (1985). *Every living thing* (pp. 73–81). New York: Aladdin. [Paperback collection of short stories.]

were they special words to you? What were some words that you thought were interesting or exciting?

b. **Feelings:** What feelings did you get when you read the story? What feelings do you think the characters had? What happened in the story to tell you how the characters were feeling? Why do you think you had the feelings that you did?

c. **Ideas:** What was the main idea of the story? What were some of the other ideas the author was trying to talk about? What was she saying about being lonely? What was she saying about differences between people? What was she saying about change?

d. **Images:** What were some of the pictures that came to your mind as you read the story? What were some things about the story that may have had more than one meaning? Why was the hermit crab important? Why was its shell important?

3. Begin a Venn diagram as a class. Draw two large, intersecting circles on the board, labeling one "Michael" and the other "Aunt Esther." Invite students to point out things that are similar about the two characters to write in the intersection of the circles and things that are different to write in the separate parts of the circles. Have students complete the diagram on paper in small groups.

4. Discuss the story, using the following questions as a guide:

Literary Response and Interpretation Questions

▼ *What is a main idea in this story?*

▼ *In what ways was Aunt Esther like the crab? In what ways was Michael?*

▼ *What does the title mean? Is it talking about just one thing or more than one thing? Explain.*

▼ *What does the phrase "came out of its shell" mean? What does it mean when it talks about a crab? What does it mean when it talks about a person? How can it apply to this story?*

▼ *At the end of the story, why does the author talk about the talc fragrance Michael smelled on Aunt Esther? Why is it important?*

Reasoning Questions

▼ *What is the problem in the story?*

▼ *What evidence or information is there in the story to support the idea that Michael and Aunt Esther are afraid of each other?*

▼ *How does the concept or idea of loneliness apply to the story?*

▼ *What do you think has changed in Michael and Aunt Esther's relationship at the end of the story? What else may change? What in the story supports your ideas?*

Change Questions

▼ *What do you think the author thinks about change in the story?*

▼ *Which of the five ideas about change does this story best support?*

5. As a whole class activity, complete the first row of the **Change Matrix** (Handout 3B). This may be laid out on butcher paper or posterboard and should remain on display in the classroom throughout the unit. The completed grid will serve as the basis for a discussion in a later lesson about change. Students should also keep copies of the Change Matrix in their notebooks.

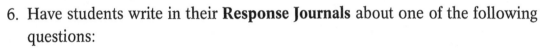

6. Have students write in their **Response Journals** about one of the following questions:

▼ *How did Michael feel about losing his parents? Give at least three sentences from the story that support your point of view.*

▼ *Michael's parents had died and his "heart hurt." Describe a situation in your life in which your "heart hurt."*

NOTES TO TEACHER

1. *The Literature Web is described in detail in the implementation section at the end of the unit. The questions indicated in this lesson to guide development of Literature Web responses may be modified and used for each Literature Web activity throughout the unit.*

2. *A fifth cell of the Literature Web asks students to comment on the structure of language as employed in the piece. Depending on student facility with the activity, this last element may be introduced at any time during the unit, using the complete model from the implementation section. Lesson 17 provides a good opportunity for students to begin to explore structure in a piece of literature.*

HOMEWORK

Write about an incident in your life when you came out of your shell. What caused it? How did you behave?

EXTENSIONS

1. Read another story by Cynthia Rylant from her collection *Every Living Thing*. Compare and contrast the young person portrayed in that story to Michael by making a Venn diagram that shows similarities and differences. Write a paragraph explaining how the two characters changed in their stories.

2. Write a paragraph arguing that people change for the better if they are encouraged or helped. Give three reasons for your point of view.

Literature Web—Teacher Example
(See Section III, Implementation, for full explanation)

Key Words
complaining
alone
fear
hermit crab
surpise

Feelings
hate
loneliness
grief
understanding

Reading

"Shells"
by
Cynthia Rylant

Ideas
loyalty
death
prejudice
growth

*Images or
Symbols*
shells
remembered
smells

Stucture (optional)

dialogue
short story
short paragraphs

Literature Web—
Primary Adaptation
(Handout 3A)

NAME: _____ DATE: _____

Key Words

Feelings

Reading

Ideas

Images or
Symbols

Change Matrix

(Handout 3B)

NAME: _____ DATE: _____

Literature	Changes in characters	Changes in setting	Changes in relationships	Change in you as a result of reading
"Shells"				
The Green Book				
Poems				
"The Ugly Duckling"				
Bringing the Rain to Kapiti Plain				
Sachiko Means Happiness				
The Green Man				
Your own story				

LESSON

4

▼

Studying Vocabulary

CURRICULUM ALIGNMENT CODE					
GOAL 1	GOAL 2	GOAL 3	GOAL 4	GOAL 5	GOAL 6
	X	X	X		

INSTRUCTIONAL PURPOSE

▼ To study vocabulary from "The Wolf and the Lion" and "Shells."

▼ To introduce learning centers.

MATERIALS USED

1. Vocabulary Web—Teacher Example

2. Vocabulary Web (Handout 4A)

3. "Shells" and "The Wolf and the Lion"

4. Dictionaries [Recommended dictionary: *American Heritage dictionary of the English language*. (3rd ed.). (1992). Boston: Houghton-Mifflin.]

5. Classroom set of *The Green Book** (Assigned as Homework)

ACTIVITIES

[PART ONE OF LESSON]

1. Introduce a **Vocabulary Web**. Put students in groups of no more than four, with a dictionary available as a resource in each group. Distribute copies of a blank Vocabulary Web and ask students to write the word *shepherd* in the center. Recall the story "The Wolf and the Lion" and ask for an explanation of what the word means. Have students find the word in the story and write the sentence in which it is found in the "Sentence" cell of the Vocabulary Web.

---

*Walsh, J. P. (1982). *The green book*. New York: Farrar Straus Giroux. [Paperback edition Farrar Straus Giroux, 1986.]

2. Ask students to look in their dictionaries to find the definition of the word. Display an enlarged copy of the definition on the board or overhead. Have students write the definition relevant to the story into the "Definition" cell of the Vocabulary Web.

3. Have students develop in their groups their own sentences using the word. Ask them to write the sentence in the "Example" cell.

4. Discuss the meanings of the words *synonym* and *antonym*. Have students check the dictionary and think about possible synonyms and antonyms for the word and fill them into the appropriate cells. (Note: Not all cells must be filled for all words; there may not be synonyms and antonyms for the words studied.)

5. Ask students what is meant by the phrase "part of speech." Have them locate the part of the dictionary definition that identifies a word's part of speech. Students should then write the part of speech for the word *shepherd* into their group webs.

6. Encourage students to think about the *stems* of the word, or the smaller words and pieces of words from which the larger word is made. Encourage them to check the dictionary for possible stems. Write any identified stems into the appropriate cell of the Vocabulary Web.

7. Have students locate the origin of the word (Latin, French, Greek, etc.) in the definition and write it in the "Origin" cell of the Vocabulary Web.

8. Ask students to think of other words in the same family as the word *shepherd*, or other words which use one or more of the same stems, and write them in the "Word Families" cell. Encourage them to use their ideas from the stems cell to give them ideas.

9. Have students continue working in small groups to complete another Vocabulary Web, using one of the following words from "The Wolf and the Lion": *lair, excuse, injure, inconvenience, evil;* or one of the following words from "Shells": *dully, fiercely, dramatic, linoleum, condominium, inherit, founding father, stupor, phenomenon, Presbyterian.*

10. Discuss the Vocabulary Webs developed by the student groups.

[PART TWO OF LESSON]

11. Introduce students to the first four unit **Learning Centers**. Learning Centers should be set up and made available for student use throughout the course of the unit; they will be introduced as they become relevant to the aspects of the unit being studied. Explain to students that the first of these Centers will give them

opportunities for more practice with the Vocabulary Web they have just learned to use, while the second will allow them to explore other aspects of language. Give each group of students a task card from the Language Study Center to complete as a way of introducing them to the Center (see below).

Learning Centers may be managed as the teacher sees fit, with specific times assigned to Center activities or on a less structured basis. Some recording system should be established for each Center, whether students will keep records in their own unit notebooks or in a notebook to be left at the Center. Additional Centers will be introduced in later lessons. (See Lessons 5, 10, and 13.)

a. Unit Vocabulary Center

At this Learning Center, a list of new vocabulary words encountered in the unit readings should be kept and regularly updated. (See Introduction to Section II for complete list.) Dictionaries and blank copies of the Vocabulary Web should be kept at the Center, as well as copies of student readings. Students visiting the Center may work alone or in small groups to develop Vocabulary Webs from unit vocabulary words, either compiling individual notebooks of webs or a class notebook. This Center allows students to gain more practice with the Vocabulary Web and to learn additional words, as class time will not allow all of the new words to be studied in depth.

b. Language Study Center

This Learning Center is intended to provide students with additional opportunities to study language. A set of task cards should be kept at the Center with short projects for students; they may keep a record in their notebooks of task card responses. Task cards may include several activities with different levels of difficulty, and points or scores may be assigned accordingly if the teacher so chooses. Some task cards may be activities students can complete on their own in the classroom, others might be small group activities, and others might require some work outside of class. Several sample task cards are listed below.

Card 1a. *The words "hear" and "here" sound the same but are spelled differently. These word pairs are called* **homophones** *or* **homonyms.** *Make a list of 20 different pairs of homophones. Can you think of a triple of homophones? A quadruple of homophones?*

Card 1b. *Complete a Vocabulary Web for the word* **homophone.**

Card 1c. *Use each pair of homophones in a single sentence.*

Card 1d. *Write silly sentences in which the meanings of two homophones are confused.*

Card 2a. *Look up the word "horrible" in three different dictionaries. How do the definitions compare? Did any of the dictionaries give additional information that was not given in the others?*

Card 2b. *Write a story in which you use the word "horrible" with each of the different meanings you found.*

Card 3. *Print the following sentence on a card:*

My cousins do not come to visit very often.

Ask at least 10 people to read it out loud. Notice how they say the word "often." Count how many pronounce the "t" and how many make it a silent "t." Check a dictionary for advice on pronunciation.

Card 4a. *In many words in the English language, we do not pronounce all of the letters we use to spell words. Write ten words which have a silent vowel and ten words which have a silent consonant.*

Card 4b. *See how many words you can write that have both a silent vowel and a silent consonant.*

Card 4c. *Put your "silent letter words" into categories. Can you see any patterns? Write a rule for each pattern that you see.*

Card 5a. *We have many different color words in our language. Make a chart of color words and find at least three different words for red, three for blue, and three for yellow.*

Card 5b. *Find the different color words in the dictionary and write explanations of how they are different.*

c. **Reading Center**

Short stories, poems, picture books, and chapter books may be made available at the Reading Center. These books may include those listed in the bibliography of extension readings as well as other materials. Students may keep a log of which pieces they have read, and may choose from a variety of assignments to complete based on their readings. Blank copies of the **Change Model** (Handout 2A) should be kept at this Center for students to fill in with examples from the stories that they read. Students may also write paragraphs to describe how the characters in a story changed or how the students themselves changed from reading the stories. New vocabulary words encountered in stories may be written in student notebooks for later exploration at the Vocabulary Web Center. The Reading Center may also serve as a small group discussion area in which students may talk about books they are reading with one another.

d. Listening Center

The Listening Center should have audio-taped books available for students, such as Joseph Bruchac's collection of Iroquois stories. As at the Reading Center, students should keep logs of what they hear, and may complete similar assignments to those listed above for the Reading Center. In addition, musical selections may be made available at the Listening Center. Question cards which emphasize the role of change in the music may be developed for these selections, including emphasis on how changes in the music can make the listener feel differently. Students may also write stories or poems based on the images created for them by the musical selections.

NOTES TO TEACHER

1. *The Vocabulary Web model is also explained in the implementation section at the end of the unit. The lesson as outlined above should be modified as appropriate based on student facility with the dictionary. This may be a time for introduction of dictionary skills, in which case teachers may choose to eliminate some of the cells of the Vocabulary Web until later; or it may be a chance for students already familiar with dictionary work to begin exploring words more deeply.*

2. *In addition to modifying this lesson as needed, teachers should carefully examine each vocabulary word to be assigned in order to assist students with the Vocabulary Webs. Some cells of the web may not be applicable to some words.*

3. *The Learning Centers for the unit are also detailed in the implementation section. Teachers may wish to introduce one or more of the Centers at a different point in the unit than indicated here.*

HOMEWORK

1. Write a new title for the story "Shells." Give two reasons for your new title.

2. Begin reading Chapters 1–2 in *The Green Book*. After you read, write a question about something that puzzles or bothers you or something you wonder about in the story. (Note: This book will not be discussed in class until Lesson 7; teachers may wish to structure homework assignment accordingly.)

EXTENSIONS

1. Research interesting vocabulary words using the format of the Vocabulary Web as a model.

2. If you enjoyed "Shells," you may enjoy reading other books by Cynthia Rylant:

   Rylant, C. (1988). *All I see.* New York: Orchard.

   Rylant, C. (1992). *An angel for Solomon Singer.* New York: Orchard.

   Rylant, C. (1991). *Appalachia: The voices of sleeping birds.* San Diego: Harcourt Brace Jovanovich.

   Rylant, C. (1983). *Miss Maggie.* New York: Dutton.

   Rylant, C. (1985). *The relatives came.* New York: Bradbury.

3. Argue for or against the effectiveness of the title of the book you chose to read from the list above. Write a paragraph telling what you thought of the title, giving at least three good reasons for your opinion, and writing a conclusion.

4. Suggest new titles for several books you have read. Give two reasons for each of your title ideas.

Vocabulary Web—Teacher Example

(See Section III, Implementation, for full explanation)

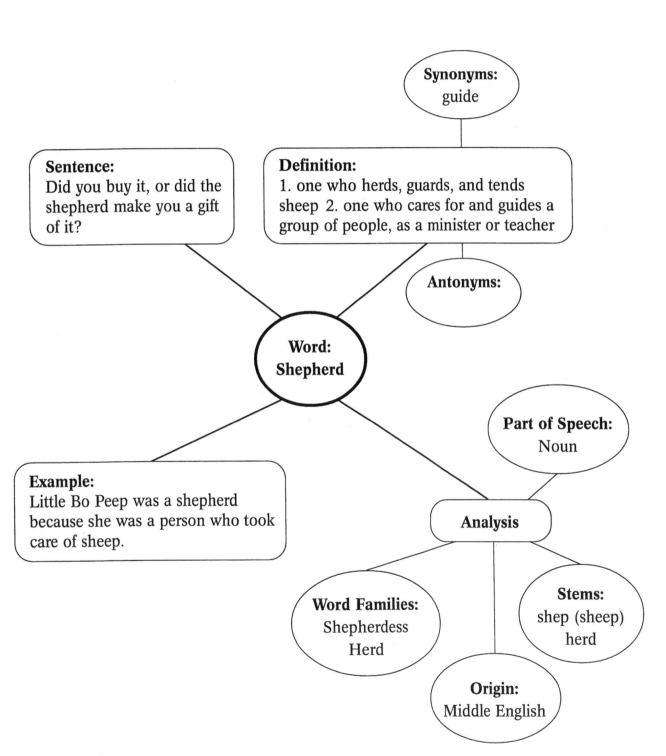

Synonyms:
guide

Sentence:
Did you buy it, or did the shepherd make you a gift of it?

Definition:
1. one who herds, guards, and tends sheep 2. one who cares for and guides a group of people, as a minister or teacher

Antonyms:

Word:
Shepherd

Part of Speech:
Noun

Example:
Little Bo Peep was a shepherd because she was a person who took care of sheep.

Analysis

Word Families:
Shepherdess
Herd

Origin:
Middle English

Stems:
shep (sheep)
herd

JOURNEYS
AND
DESTINATIONS

Vocabulary Web
(Handout 4A)

NAME: _____ DATE: _____

Synonyms:

Sentence:

Definition:

Antonyms:

Word:

Part of Speech:

Example:

Analysis

Word Families:

Stems:

Origin:

LESSON

5

▼

Persuasive Writing with the Hamburger Model

CURRICULUM ALIGNMENT CODE

GOAL 1	GOAL 2	GOAL 3	GOAL 4	GOAL 5	GOAL 6
	X				

INSTRUCTIONAL PURPOSE

▼ To introduce persuasive writing through use of the Hamburger Model.

MATERIALS USED

1. Hamburger Model of Persuasive Writing (Handout 5A)

2. Example of a Hamburger Paragraph (Handout 5B)

3. Jumbled Paragraph (Handout 5C)

ACTIVITIES

1. Introduce the **Hamburger Model of Persuasive Writing** (Handout 5A). Tell students that it is not the only way to write a paragraph but that it will work well to help them write the kind of paragraph they were asked to write for the pre-assessment activity. Share the **Example Hamburger Paragraph** (Handout 5B). Discuss the parts of the model as found in the paragraph.

2. Give out the **Jumbled Paragraph** (Handout 5C) to small groups of students. Have them cut the sentences apart and rearrange the pieces using the Hamburger Model as a guide. Have a volunteer share the group product with the whole class. Discuss the reasoning that helped unscramble the paragraph.

3. Discuss the effectiveness of the paragraph by putting a copy on the overhead projector. Have students volunteer to circle the "top bun," the "bottom bun," and the "meat" of the paragraph.

4. Help the class write a hamburger paragraph arguing from the point of view of a parent who does *not* think it is a good idea to have a dog as a pet. After starting as a whole class, students may work in small groups to complete the paragraph. Have a group volunteer to share with the whole group and put together a paragraph on the overhead projector.

5. Introduce the next **Learning Center** for the unit.

   Writing/Computer Center

   At this Learning Center, students have the opportunity to practice the stages of writing and the format of the persuasive paragraph. Writing materials and a word processing program should be made available to students, along with a list of suggested writing topics. Students may compose paragraphs and longer pieces at the Writing/Computer Center, may work in pairs to critique one another's work, and may revise, edit, and publish their work. This Center may be used to work on unit assignments and/or on separate extension activities.

NOTES TO TEACHER

1. *The Hamburger Model is also explained in the implementation section at the end of the unit. It may be helpful to keep an enlarged copy of the Model posted in the classroom for reference throughout the unit.*

2. *Here is the key to the Jumbled Paragraph:*

   I think that we should consider getting a dog for a pet. First, it would help me learn to be responsible. I would have to feed it and take it for a walk every day. Second, it would keep me company when there is no one else to play with. It would also scare away strangers who are up to no good. So you see, having a dog for a pet would be a good thing for our family.

HOMEWORK

Write a hamburger paragraph to answer this question: "Should students in our grade take physical education every school day?" Make sure you include a top bun, plenty of meat or veggies, and a bottom bun.

EXTENSIONS

Explore transitional words. Make a list of words that can be used to signal changes in sentences or paragraphs at different stages of a paragraph. Examples: **then, finally, at first, next**.

Hamburger Model of Persuasive Writing

(Handout 5A)

NAME: _____ DATE: _____

Introduction
(State your opinion.)

Elaboration Elaboration Elaboration

Reasons Reasons Reasons

Elaboration Elaboration Elaboration

Conclusion

Example Hamburger Paragraph
(Handout 5B)

NAME: _____ DATE: _____

I don't think students should be given homework on the weekends. They have too many other things to do. They have worked hard the other nights of the week and need a break. Most homework is just busy work anyway. Overall, it is not a good idea to give homework on weekends.

Jumbled Paragraph

(Handout 5C)

NAME: _____ DATE: _____

Directions: Cut the sentences apart and rearrange them to form a good hamburger paragraph.

Dog vs. No Dog

I would have to feed it and take it for a walk every day.

It would also scare away strangers who are up to no good.

I think that we should consider getting a dog for a pet.

Second, it would keep me company when there is no one else to play with.

So you see, having a dog for a pet would be a good thing for our family.

First, it would help me learn to be responsible.

LESSON

6

Writing and Thinking

CURRICULUM ALIGNMENT CODE

GOAL 1	GOAL 2	GOAL 3	GOAL 4	GOAL 5	GOAL 6
	X			X	

INSTRUCTIONAL PURPOSE

▼ To introduce elements of reasoning as a part of persuasive writing.

MATERIALS USED

1. Hamburger Model (Handout 5A)
2. Example of a Hamburger Paragraph (Handout 5B)
3. Elements of Reasoning (Overhead 6A)
4. Standards of Reasoning (Handout 6B)
5. Sample Paragraph (Handout 6C)

ACTIVITIES

1. Return to the **Example Paragraph** from the last lesson (Handout 5B). Ask students if they find the arguments convincing, or if they think the paragraph would be enough to make teachers stop giving homework on the weekends. Ask for suggestions in strengthening the arguments/reasons.

2. Explain that the hamburger structure alone does not guarantee a strong persuasive paragraph. One needs to look carefully at the information and reasons that make up the *ideas* of the paragraph. Show the **Elements of Reasoning** (Handout 6A) on the overhead projector. Explain that these elements can help us think and argue better, and that we will begin paying attention to some of them carefully in our writing to make our Hamburger Paragraphs even better.

3. Return to the **Hamburger Model** (Handout 5A). Overlay "point of view" and "issue" on the top bun, "evidence" in the middle, and "consequences" in the bottom bun. Use the following questions to help students see the relationship of persuasive writing to these elements of reasoning:

   ▼ *What do you think is meant by **point of view**? What is the point of view of the writer in the paragraph about homework on the weekends? What other point of view might someone take? (teacher, parents, principal)*

   ▼ *What do you think is meant by an **issue**? What is the issue in the example paragraph? What other issues have we used in paragraphs?*

   ▼ *What do you think is meant by **evidence**? What is the evidence that is given in the example paragraph? Are there enough supporting details to make a good argument?*

   ▼ *What do you think is meant by **consequences**? What are the consequences of having homework every weekend? What are the consequences of never having homework? What difference does it make to your family if you get a dog?*

4. In order to judge the quality of the reasoning, introduce **Standards of Reasoning** (Handout 6B) by using the questions below. Have students discuss their answers to these questions based on the example paragraph given:

   ▼ *Are there **enough reasons** to make a convincing argument? One or two reasons might not be enough to show someone your point of view well enough for them to understand it.*

   ▼ *Is the evidence **correct or right**? Teachers might not agree that "Most of the homework is busy work."*

   ▼ *Are the reasons **clear**? Is the meaning understandable by anyone who reads this?*

   ▼ *Are **specific** reasons or examples included rather than vague generalizations? "It would help me learn to be responsible" alone is too general. "I would have to feed it and take it for a walk every day" is more specific and helps strengthen the argument in the dog paragraph. How specific are the reasons in the homework paragraph?*

   ▼ *Are the arguments and reasons **strong and important**, or do they seem to be included just to have something to say?*

▼ *Is the thinking **logical**? Does the paragraph follow an understandable path or is it just a disconnected group of statements? Do the sentences seem to go together and to be in the right order?*

5. With the whole class, examine the **Sample Paragraph** (Handout 6C). Which of the standards of reasoning are reflected in the paragraph? Give students copies of the questions on Handout 6B and discuss how they may be answered with regard to the paragraph on Handout 6C.

6. Give small groups five minutes to jot down ideas for a paragraph to answer the following question:

   Should recess be after lunch or at the end of the school day?

   Have them share ideas in their groups and then ask for volunteers to contribute parts in order to write a class paragraph on the overhead projector. Examine the paragraph structure using the Hamburger Model and the strength of the reasons by using the questions in Handout 6B.

NOTE TO TEACHER

The Elements of Reasoning are explained in detail in the implementation section at the end of the unit. Depending on student readiness level, teachers may wish to introduce more or fewer elements than those emphasized in this lesson. Teachers should also modify Handout 6B (Standards of Reasoning) to reflect which elements will be emphasized in class.

HOMEWORK

Write a hamburger paragraph on the following topic by writing a letter to the editor of your school paper:

Should students be required to wear seatbelts on buses?

Make sure it is in the form of a hamburger paragraph and that the reasons you use to support your point of view are strong according to our earlier discussion of the standards of reasoning.

EXTENSIONS

1. Look for examples of persuasive arguments on editorial pages of newspapers or magazines. Analyze the arguments using the question list from Handout 6B.

2. **To the Teacher:** For students who are ready, suggest that they acknowledge another point of view in their argument. Ask, "Have you thought about what somebody with another point of view would say?" Ask this additional question concerning the standards for reasoning: Is this a *fair* treatment of the issue? or is it biased or one-sided?

3. Explore the element of reasoning called "purpose." Work with a few other students to discuss your purpose in several pieces of writing.

4. **To the Teacher:** Introduce *logical reasoning* activities. Use the *Mind Benders* series (Harnadek, A. *Mind Benders*. Pacific Grove, CA: Critical Thinking Books & Software) or other deductive thinking resources to get students to explore logical reasoning. (Note: Logical thinking task cards may be added to the Language Study Center or be included in a Learning Center of their own.)

JOURNEYS
AND
DESTINATIONS

Elements of Reasoning
(Overhead 6A)

Purpose or Goal

Issue or Problem

Point of View

Experiences, Data, or Evidence

Concepts or Ideas

Assumptions

Inferences

Implications and Consequences

Standards for Reasoning
(Handout 6B)

NAME: _____ DATE: _____

Use these questions to think about the reasoning used in a hamburger paragraph:

▼ Are there **enough reasons** to make a convincing argument? One or two reasons might not be enough to show someone your point of view well enough for them to understand it.

▼ Is the evidence **correct or right**? Teachers might not agree that "Most of the homework is busy work."

▼ Are the reasons **clear**? Is the meaning understandable by anyone who reads this?

▼ Are **specific** reasons or examples included rather than vague generalizations? "It would help me learn to be responsible" alone is too general. "I would have to feed it and take it for a walk every day" is more specific and helps strengthen the argument in the dog paragraph. How specific are the reasons in the homework paragraph?

▼ Are the arguments and reasons **strong and important**, or do they seem to be included just to have something to say?

▼ Is the thinking **logical**? Does the paragraph follow an understandable path or is it just a disconnected group of statements? Do the sentences seem to go together and to be in the right order?

Sample Paragraph

(Handout 6C)

NAME: _____ DATE: _____

Teacher Response to Homework on the Weekend

I believe that students should be assigned a small amount of homework on weekends. Studies show that regular homework provides the practice that students need to master basic skills such as math and reading. Four nights a week is not enough to keep their skills up. Some assignments such as reading novels or getting library sources for a report require a longer period of time to complete. Students are very busy during the week with sports, music lessons, and clubs, and they often have early bedtimes on school nights. The weekend gives a little more time to complete assignments. I think that the overall benefits of homework on the weekend outweigh the inconvenience to students.

LESSON

7

The Green Book

CURRICULUM ALIGNMENT CODE

GOAL 1	GOAL 2	GOAL 3	GOAL 4	GOAL 5	GOAL 6
X	X	X		X	X

INSTRUCTIONAL PURPOSE

▼ To develop reasoning skills in literature through discussion of *The Green Book*.

▼ To explore new vocabulary words.

MATERIALS USED

1. Classroom set of *The Green Book*

2. Literature Web—Primary Adaptation (Handout 7A)

3. Vocabulary Web (Handout 7B)

4. Student Response Journals

5. *Mission to Deep Space: Voyagers' Journey of Discovery* by W. E. Burrows

6. Assorted magazines

ACTIVITIES

1. Complete a whole class **Literature Web** (Handout 7A) on Chapters 1–2 in *The Green Book*, again discussing each piece of the web with specific references to the text. See Lesson 3 for sample guiding questions for each cell of the web.

2. Have students do a "Read-Around Activity" based on the questions they wrote about the book for homework. This activity offers students an opportunity to ask authentic questions and to answer the questions of their classmates. Divide the class into groups of five. Ask students to use the questions they wrote for home-

work in Lesson 4 or additional questions they have about *The Green Book* for this activity. Remind them that the questions should not be simply recall questions from the story, but real "thinking" questions.

Each student should write a question on a sheet of paper and pass it to the left. Each student will then answer the question he or she received in two to four sentences, writing immediately under the question. When students are finished answering, they pass the question once more to the left; the next student reads the question and the answer, then writes a different answer or explains why he/she agrees with the first student's answer. The questions are then returned to their authors. Each student reads the question and the two answers.

After students have read their original questions and the answers they received, share the questions and answers. Discuss how the process changed the students' understanding of the story.

3. Discuss the book, using the following questions.

Literary Response and Interpretation Questions

▼ *Why are these people leaving the Earth?*

▼ *Why doesn't the author give a name to the new planet?*

▼ *On page 11, what does Joe mean when he says, "Oh, Pattie! You're a fine one to talk about choosing!"*

▼ *What surprises do the travelers find on the new planet?*

Reasoning Questions

▼ *What issues and questions are raised by the children about their new home on page 10? (e.g., Can the planet support life?)*

▼ *What do you know about who the people are on the spaceship? What evidence tells you that?*

▼ *What assumptions or guesses did the children make about the grass and flowers before they ran forward (on page 17)?*

Change Questions

▼ *What does the paragraph about games on pages 6–7 tell us about change?*

4. Have students work in groups to complete a **Vocabulary Web** (Handout 7B) for one of the following words from *The Green Book*: **rations, p. 3; perishable, p. 3; wistfully, p. 4; treacle, p. 4; allocated, p. 7; runnel, p. 16; rivulet, p. 18;** and

flagons, p. 18. (Note: This activity may be done as a whole class, depending on student facility with the Vocabulary Web. See Lesson 4 for guidance in Vocabulary Web development.)

5. Introduce the **Lightning Round** as a vocabulary review activity. Divide students into two or more teams. Give one member of each team a buzzer or a bell. The game moderator, who may be the teacher or a student, reads aloud a definition of one of the words studied thus far in the unit. The students holding buzzers may signal if they know to what word the definition refers. Other team members are silent, and helping is not allowed. The person who buzzes in first is called on by the moderator to respond, giving the answer in the form of a question. (Example: "What is a shepherd?") If the correct response is given, the team earns a point. If it is incorrect, a member from another team is called on to give the correct response. After a correct response has been recorded the buzzer of each team is then passed on to the team member on the right. This process is repeated until all definitions for unit words studied so far have been called and the game is over.

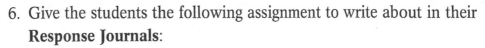

6. Give the students the following assignment to write about in their **Response Journals**:

   ▼ *Imagine that you are going on the voyage to the new planet. Decide what book you would choose to take along. Give several reasons for your choice.*

7. Have students make a **Venn Diagram** showing how the environments of the Earth and the new planet are the same and different. This diagram may include pictures as well as words to describe the two planets.

8. Introduce the book *Mission to Deep Space: Voyagers' Journey of Discovery* by William E. Burrows (1993), which offers a fascinating scientific parallel to the science fiction of *The Green Book*. Of particular interest, it provides a list of items placed on the Voyager spacecrafts intended to represent the planet Earth and to serve as a greeting to intelligent beings of the universe. Explore the idea of creating such collections, in this context and in the "time capsule" context. Have students work in groups to determine aspects of life in their place and time which they think should be represented in a time capsule (e.g., technology, music, art, architecture, literature, family and educational systems, etc.). Then assign each group one of these areas, and have students create a collage of pictures from magazines of specific items they might include in the time capsule for their topic area. Have the groups then write a description of the items chosen and why they were selected as representative of the time and culture.

NOTE TO TEACHER

The Lightning Round introduced in this lesson may be used as a vocabulary review activity throughout the unit, and should provide a culminating vocabulary activity in Lesson 22.

HOMEWORK

1. Ask at least two members of your family what book each of them would choose to take if they were on the trip to the new planet. Ask each of them to give reasons for the choice. Write their responses to bring to class for discussion.

2. Read Chapters 3–4 in *The Green Book*.

EXTENSIONS

1. On page 19 Joe sets up a calendar. How does it work? What determines a day on the new planet? Do you think it is the same length as a day on Earth? Explain. Find out more about the lengths of days and years on planets in our solar system. Why are they different from each other?

2. It took four years for the spacecraft to travel to the new planet. How far away from Earth might that be? How can you find out?

Literature Web—
Primary Adaptation
(Handout 7A)

NAME: _____ DATE: _____

Key Words

Feelings

Reading

Ideas

Images or
Symbols

JOURNEYS AND DESTINATIONS

Vocabulary Web
(Handout 7B)

NAME: _____ DATE: _____

Synonyms:

Sentence:

Definition:

Antonyms:

Word:

Part of Speech:

Example:

Analysis

Word Families:

Stems:

Origin:

8

William Shakespeare and *The Green Book*

CURRICULUM ALIGNMENT CODE

GOAL 1	GOAL 2	GOAL 3	GOAL 4	GOAL 5	GOAL 6
X	X	X		X	X

INSTRUCTIONAL PURPOSE

▼ To develop reasoning skills in literature through discussion of *The Green Book*.

▼ To explore new vocabulary words.

▼ To encourage and develop persuasive writing skills.

MATERIALS USED

1. Classroom set of *The Green Book*

2. Literature Web—Primary Adaptation (Handout 8A)

3. Vocabulary Web (Handout 8B)

4. Student Response Journals

5. Writing Assignment (Handout 8C)

6. Shakespeare Quotes (Handout 8D)

ACTIVITIES

1. Have students work in pairs to complete a **Literature Web** (Handout 8A) on their reading of Chapters 3–4 in *The Green Book* in order to focus their thoughts before the following discussion.

2. Begin discussion, using the following questions.

Literary Response and Interpretation Questions

▼ *On page 38, what does Father mean when he says, "We will be very respectable citizens here"?*

▼ *Why does Father say, "Not one Shakespeare . . . among us all, not one"?*

▼ *Why do the adults begin calling each other brother and sister?*

▼ *What is the importance of the line on page 46 that says, "Bill was the one who had Homer"?*

▼ *Why does Bill ask for payment for people to read his book?*

▼ *Why does Joe tell the children not to tell anyone else about the candy trees yet?*

Reasoning Questions

▼ *How important is technology to the survival of the group on the new planet? What substitutes can they fall back on if they do not have the technology they had on Earth?*

▼ *What assumptions or guesses did people make about why Father was not helping with the seed planting?*

▼ *What assumptions or guesses did people make about choosing their books to take to the new planet? Were they correct?*

▼ *How do you think Father feels about his technology book? What in the story tells you how he feels? Why do you think he feels that way?*

▼ *What do you think the author's purpose was in writing about the candy trees on the new planet?*

Change Questions

▼ *How have things changed for the people of Shine in terms of food, technology, etc. since they arrived?*

3. Have students work in groups to complete a **Vocabulary Web** (Handout 8B) for one of the following words from *The Green Book*: ***biorhythms, p. 34; fodder, p. 38;*** and ***relevant, p. 41***.

4. Have students respond to the following question in their **Response Journals**:

> ▼ *If you were asked to choose a name for the new settlement, what would you call it? Give reasons from the book for your choice.*

5. Review the pieces of a hamburger paragraph (Lesson 5). Give students the **Writing Assignment** (Handout 8C) and invite them to brainstorm ideas for special objects to take with them if they were moving. Read the second part of the assignment and discuss how one might structure a paragraph for the assignment. Have students write a draft of a persuasive paragraph explaining why the item they have chosen would be most important to them to take.

6. Pursue the significance of Shakespeare as an author whose works are important to Father in the story. Use resources such as *Under the Greenwood Tree* and *Bard of Avon* for assistance. [Holdridge, B. (Ed.). (1986). *Under the Greenwood Tree*. Owings Mills, MD: Stemmer House; Stanley, D., & Vennema, P. (1992). *Bard of Avon*. New York: Morrow Junior Books.]

> ▼ *Bring in a copy of the complete works of Shakespeare and give a short description of what kinds of writing he did.*
>
> ▼ *Use the quotes on Handout 8D as the basis for discussion. Ask students what they think Shakespeare meant by the quotes. Have students copy the quotes and write and illustrate short stories to go with them. (Note: The word "glisters" in the quote from* The Merchant of Venice *is the correct term; it is often misquoted as "glitters.")*
>
> ▼ *Ask the question: Why do Shakespeare's plays continue to be so popular today?*
>
> ▼ *Ask students to poll parents, librarians, teachers, etc. to see if they can identify the author of these quotes (and the play from which each comes!). Have them ask these adults if they feel it is important to preserve and study the writings of Shakespeare and why.*

HOMEWORK

1. Complete draft of writing assignment.
2. Read Chapter 5 in *The Green Book*.

EXTENSIONS

1. Find out what poem Father is reciting on page 31. Read the entire poem. (**Note to Teacher:** It is "I Wandered Lonely as a Cloud," by William Wordsworth.)

2. We take some things, such as clouds, for granted. Pattie does not remember clouds. How would you explain clouds to her? If you need to, find out more information about clouds. Remember that you have the advantage of a lot of resources that Pattie's family does not have on the new planet.

Literature Web—
Primary Adaptation
(Handout 8A)

NAME: _____ DATE: _____

Key Words

Feelings

Reading

Ideas

Images or
Symbols

Vocabulary Web
(Handout 8B)

NAME: _____ DATE: _____

Synonyms:

Sentence:

Definition:

Antonyms:

Word:

Part of Speech:

Example:

Analysis

Word Families:

Stems:

Origin:

87

Writing Assignment
(Handout 8C)

NAME: _____ DATE: _____

Imagine that you are moving with your family to a new home in another state. Make a list of special objects which you have that you might take with you to help you remember a special person, place, or time.

Your parents tell you that space for moving things is very limited. Choose the most important item to take along and write a paragraph explaining why you must take it. Your paragraph should include a statement of your point of view on the issue, at least three clear reasons for your point of view, and a conclusion.

Shakespeare Quotes
(Handout 8D)

NAME: _____ DATE: _____

Neither a borrower nor a lender be,
For loan oft loses both itself and friend . . .

—*Hamlet*

All that glisters is not gold;

—*The Merchant of Venice*

See how she leans her cheek upon her hand!
O that I were a glove upon that hand
That I might touch that cheek.

—*Romeo and Juliet*

What's in a name? That which we call a rose
By any other name would smell as sweet.

—*Romeo and Juliet*

All the world's a stage,
And all the men and women merely players:
They have their exits and their entrances;
And one man in his time plays many parts,
His acts being seven ages.

—*As You Like It*

LESSON

9

The Green Book, continued

CURRICULUM ALIGNMENT CODE

GOAL 1	GOAL 2	GOAL 3	GOAL 4	GOAL 5	GOAL 6
X	X	X		X	X

INSTRUCTIONAL PURPOSE

▼ To develop reasoning skills in literature through discussion of *The Green Book*.

▼ To explore new vocabulary words.

▼ To revise student writing.

MATERIALS USED

1. Classroom set of *The Green Book*

2. Literature Web—Primary Adaptation (Handout 9A)

3. Vocabulary Web (Handout 9B)

4. Completed Writing Assignments (from Lesson 8)

5. Self-Assessment for Writing (Handout 9C)

6. Peer Assessment for Writing (Handout 9D)

7. Teacher Assessment for Writing (Handout 9E)

ACTIVITIES

1. Have students work in groups to complete a **Literature Web** (Handout 9A) on their reading of Chapter 5 in *The Green Book*.

2. Begin discussion using the following questions.

Literary Response and Interpretation Questions

▼ *On page 54, why does Pattie feel that the wheat field is more frightening than the moths?*

▼ *How and why did the people of Shine try to communicate with the moth people? How did they finally succeed in communicating?*

Reasoning Questions

▼ *What reaction do the adults have to the hatching of the moth people? What evidence tells you this?*

▼ *What assumptions do the children make about the moth people? What assumptions do the adults make?*

Change Questions

▼ *How has the people's understanding of the new planet changed within this section of the book?*

▼ *How have relationships among the people changed since they arrived on the new planet?*

▼ *What does the part of the story that describes the moth people tell us about change? How is the first description of the moth people different from descriptions later in the chapter? Why are the descriptions different? How do the descriptions help the reader understand the way the people are feeling about the moths?*

3. Have students work in groups to complete a **Vocabulary Web** (Handout 9B) for one of the following words from *The Green Book: hexagon, p. 54; hostile, p. 55; malfunction, p. 55; consciousness, p. 55.*

4. Introduce the following assignment to students: **Draw a map** of the settlement area on the new planet. Include the lake, the landing place of the spacecraft, the community of Shine, and Boulder Valley. Explain why you think each is located where you drew it. Share your maps in small groups and discuss a few as a class.

5. Introduce students to the three **Assessments for Writing** (Handouts 9C, 9D, 9E). Discuss the items included on the forms and how they relate to the Hamburger Model used to organize writing. Have students independently complete a **Self-Assessment for Writing** (Handout 9C) for the writing assignment from Lesson 8. Then have students work in groups of three to share their writing, using the **Peer Assessment for Writing** (Handout 9D) to guide the discussion. Remind

students that at this stage, they are working on revising the content and form of their writing, trying to strengthen their arguments and supporting details, rather than focusing on editing issues. Students may also conference with teachers on their writing assignment during this time, with reference to the **Teacher Assessment for Writing** (Handout 9E). (Revision of student writing may occur in groups simultaneously with the map-drawing activity or as a separate part of the day.)

HOMEWORK

1. Work on revisions of the writing assignment based on feedback from peers and teachers.

2. Read Chapters 6–7 in *The Green Book*.

EXTENSIONS

1. Find a collection of *Grimm's Fairy Tales* and read one of the stories that was mentioned in *The Green Book* (See below). Then write in your **Response Journal** about whether you think it would have been important to take it along to the new planet. Explain why or why not.

   "The Feathers"

   "The Fisherman and His Wife"

   "The Boy Who Had to Learn Fear"

2. If you were going on the voyage to the new planet and were allowed to take "one or two personal items," what would you take? Write about it in your **Response Journal** and give reasons for your choices.

3. Would the personal items you took to a new planet be the same as those you took to a new state or different? Why? Make a Venn diagram about the differences between moving to a new state and traveling to a new planet.

Literature Web—
Primary Adaptation
(Handout 9A)

NAME: _____ DATE: _____

Key Words

Feelings

Reading

Ideas

Images or
Symbols

Vocabulary Web
(Handout 9B)

NAME: _____ DATE: _____

Synonyms:

Sentence:

Definition:

Antonyms:

Word:

Part of Speech:

Example:

Analysis

Word Families:

Stems:

Origin:

Self-Assessment for Writing

(Handout 9C)

NAME: _____ DATE: _____

ASSIGNMENT: _____

Directions: Grade your own writing. For each sentence below, circle the choice that describes your writing best.

1. My main idea is clear.	Needs Improvement	Satisfactory	Excellent
2. My details support the main idea.	Needs Improvement	Satisfactory	Excellent
3. My ideas flow smoothly and orderly.	Needs Improvement	Satisfactory	Excellent
4. The hamburger paragraph structure is clear (introduction, body, conclusion).	Needs Improvement	Satisfactory	Excellent
5. My vocabulary is rich and varied.	Needs Improvement	Satisfactory	Excellent

MY WRITING IS STRONG IN THESE WAYS:

_____

_____

_____

MY WRITING COULD BE IMPROVED IN THESE WAYS:

_____

_____

_____

Peer Assessment for Writing
(Handout 9D)

READER: _____ WRITER: _____

ASSIGNMENT: _____

Directions: Read your partner's writing sample carefully. For each sentence below, circle the choice that you think describes the writing.

1. The main idea is clear.	Needs Improvement	Satisfactory	Excellent
2. The details support the main idea.	Needs Improvement	Satisfactory	Excellent
3. The ideas flow smoothly and orderly.	Needs Improvement	Satisfactory	Excellent
4. The hamburger paragraph structure is clear (introduction, body, conclusion).	Needs Improvement	Satisfactory	Excellent
5. The vocabulary is rich and varied.	Needs Improvement	Satisfactory	Excellent

THE WRITING SAMPLE IS STRONG IN THESE WAYS:

_____

_____

_____

THE WRITING SAMPLE COULD BE IMPROVED IN THESE WAYS:

_____

_____

_____

Teacher Assessment for Writing

(Handout 9E)

STUDENT: _____ DATE: _____

ASSIGNMENT: _____

Directions: Circle the words that best describe the writing.

1. The main idea is clear.	Needs Improvement	Satisfactory	Excellent
2. Appropriate level of detail is provided to support the main idea.	Needs Improvement	Satisfactory	Excellent
3. The ideas flow smoothly and orderly.	Needs Improvement	Satisfactory	Excellent
4. The hamburger paragraph structure is clear (introduction, body, conclusion).	Needs Improvement	Satisfactory	Excellent
5. The writing uses descriptive language and rich vocabulary.	Needs Improvement	Satisfactory	Excellent

Optional:

Demonstrates correct grammar, usage, and mechanics.	Needs Improvement	Satisfactory	Excellent

PARTICULAR STRENGTHS:

_____

_____

AREAS NEEDING IMPROVEMENT:

_____

_____

LESSON
10

Remembering and Research

CURRICULUM ALIGNMENT CODE

GOAL 1	GOAL 2	GOAL 3	GOAL 4	GOAL 5	GOAL 6
X	X	X		X	X

INSTRUCTIONAL PURPOSE

▼ To develop reasoning skills in literature through discussion of *The Green Book*.

▼ To explore new vocabulary words.

▼ To introduce the research model through exploring an issue.

▼ To edit student writing.

MATERIALS USED

1. Classroom set of *The Green Book*

2. Literature Web—Primary Adaptation (Handout 10A)

3. Vocabulary Web (Handout 10B)

4. Change Model (Handout 10C)

5. Change Matrix (Handout 3B; large class chart created in Lesson 3)

6. Research Assignment (Handout 10D)

7. Research Model (Handout 10E)

8. Topic Web (Handout 10F)

9. Completed Writing Assignment (from Lessons 8 and 9)

ACTIVITIES

1. Have students work in groups to complete a **Literature Web** (Handout 10A) on their reading of Chapters 6–7 in *The Green Book*.

2. Continue discussion using the following questions.

Literary Response and Interpretation Questions

▼ *How are light and fire used to make the story more interesting for the reader? Light and fire are **images** in the story; how do they help you see more of the story in your mind?*

▼ *What does the silence that is described on page 64 mean? Why is it important?*

▼ *What is the role or importance of paper in this story?*

Reasoning Questions

▼ *What assumptions has Father made about the wheat? What evidence supports this?*

▼ *How does the concept or idea of cooperation develop throughout the story? How is the group's cooperation different at the end than it was at the beginning?*

▼ *What was the goal of the people who went to the new planet? Was this goal accomplished?*

▼ *When you began reading this story, from what point of view did you assume it was being told? At the end of the story, how does your understanding of the point of view change? How important is the point of view in the telling of the story?*

Change Questions

▼ *Many things have changed for the people since they left earth, but some things have remained the same. What are some of the important changes that have happened, and what are some things that have stayed the same?*

▼ *A "change agent" is a person or thing that causes changes to occur. How are the children change agents in the story?*

3. Have students work in groups to complete a **Vocabulary Web** (Handout 10B) for one of the following words from *The Green Book*: **rapt, p. 64** and **scudding, p. 64**.

4. Provide small groups of students with copies of the **Change Model** (Handout 10C) (or have them draw a Change Model on a large sheet of paper). Have students

write or draw examples from *The Green Book* which support each of the generalizations about change. Discuss student ideas as a class.

5. As a whole class activity, complete the column of the **Change Matrix** (Handout 3B in Lesson 3; students should have copies in their notebooks) that applies to *The Green Book*. Have students complete their copy of the Matrix as well as filling in the large butcher paper or posterboard copy for classroom display. The completed grid will serve as the basis for a discussion in a later lesson about change.

6. **Remembering** is an important idea in this story. As a class do a concept map about remembering. Write the word "remembering" on a large sheet of paper and discuss what remembering means, examples of remembering, and other ideas about remembering, writing the ideas on the paper so that they branch out from the central concept. Use the questions below as a guide.

   ▼ *What kinds of things are important to remember? What things are important to remember at school? What things are important to remember about people we care about? What does it mean to "keep a memory alive"?*

   ▼ *In what ways do we help ourselves remember? How do you remember information for tests? How do you remember stories?*

   ▼ *Do we want to remember everything? What might be some things we would wish to forget?*

   ▼ *Think about the people on the new planet and what they would find important to remember about life on Earth. How might they keep their memories of Earth alive?*

7. Introduce and discuss the **Research Assignment** for the unit (Handout 10D). Review the **Research Model** students will use to design their projects (Handout 10E). The steps of the research process demonstrate how to use a variety of resources to build understanding and to form a point of view. As a class, discuss the first step in the research model, the identification of the issue or problem. Have students brainstorm a few questions related to the issue. Divide students into small groups and distribute **Topic Webs** (Handout 10F). Encourage the groups to continue brainstorming questions and possible resources for accessing information, working in the top two cells of the Topic Web. Have students share their group ideas with the class and discuss. Explain that students will work on the research assignment throughout the unit, gathering information to answer their questions from the different sources. Compile the class ideas of possible questions and information sources and post in the classroom for reference.

8. Have students work in pairs to read one another's revised writing assignments from Lessons 8 and 9 for editing. Students may also consult with the teacher about editing questions, and may use a spell-check on a computer when publishing written work. After editing comments have been made, students should write a final copy of their work to be posted on a bulletin board or included in a class booklet.

9. Introduce the next **Learning Center** for the unit:

Research Center

This Learning Center may include a regular and an electronic encyclopedia, nonfiction books such as those listed in "Notes to Teacher," below, and other resources which will help students in investigating their issue. A list of guiding questions and key terms to investigate may help students in their research efforts. In addition, this Center may include nonfiction materials about the authors whose works are included in the unit as well as the people, places, and things described in the readings, so that students may pursue areas of interest.

NOTES TO TEACHER

1. *The research issue presented in this unit should generate much discussion of technologies such as videotapes, various cameras, and computers. Encourage students to think of such equipment as ways of preserving memories and to discuss how memories were preserved before such items existed. Relate such discussion back to* The Green Book, *considering how memories could be preserved if the technology on which we rely were to be taken from us.*

2. *The following books provide excellent background material for this research project*

   "Faces." (1996, February). Special issue. *Faces*. Cobblestone.

   Jean, G. (1992). *Writing: The story of alphabets and scripts* (trans. J. Oates). New York: Harry N. Abrams.

   Lubar, S. (1993). *InfoCulture: The Smithsonian book of information age inventions*. Boston: Houghton Mifflin.

   Knight, M. B. (1992). *Talking walls*. Gardiner, ME: Tilbary House.

   Myers, W. P. (1993). *Brown angels: An album of pictures and verse*. New York: HarperCollins.

HOMEWORK

1. Complete final copy of writing assignment.

2. Begin locating resources for the research assignment.

3. Bring two photographs of yourself to the next class session. One photograph should be a recent one, while another should be from when you were younger (for example, you may bring a photo from preschool or kindergarten).

EXTENSION

Watch a half-hour news program and take notes on the three most important stories covered. Why do you think those three are most important?

Literature Web—
Primary Adaptation
(Handout 10A)

NAME: _____ DATE: _____

Key Words

Feelings

Reading

Ideas

Images or
Symbols

Vocabulary Web

(Handout 10B)

NAME: _____ DATE: _____

Synonyms:

Sentence:

Definition:

Antonyms:

Word:

Part of Speech:

Example:

Analysis

Word Families:

Stems:

Origin:

115

Change Model
(Handout 10C)

NAME: _____ DATE: _____

Change is linked to time:

Change is everywhere:

Change

Change may be positive:

. . . or negative:

Change may be perceived as orderly:

. . . or random:

Change may happen naturally:

or may be caused by people:

Research Assignment

(Handout 10D)

NAME: _____ DATE: _____

Over the years there have been many ways to preserve memories, or to keep important things from being forgotten. Brainstorm some of the ways people preserve memories. How many can you think of? (diaries, photograph albums, paintings and drawings, stories, video tapes, books, audio tape recordings, religious festivals and rituals, initials carved in trees, museum collections, libraries, copy machines, etc.) Which of these ways require technology such as electricity? Divide your list into two groups—traditional methods that do not depend on technology and modern methods that use technology. What are the advantages and disadvantages of each type?

Choose a point of view about the best ways to preserve memories. Do some research to support your point of view. Your research might include library materials, interviews, or a poll.

Later in this unit you will write a short paper (one to two pages) and give a two-minute presentation on your point of view, supported by your findings. You will write this paper using the Hamburger Model, just as you have practiced work paragraphs in class.

Research Model
(Handout 10E)

NAME: _____ DATE: _____

1. **Identify your issue or problem.**

   What is the issue or problem?

   Who are the stakeholders and what are their positions?

   What is *your* position on this issue?

2. **Read about your issue and identify points of view or arguments through information sources.**

   What are my print sources?

   What are my media sources?

   What are my people sources?

   What are my preliminary findings based on a review of existing sources?

3. **Form a set of questions that can be answered by people you would like to interview who understand the issue or problem.**

   My Interview Questions:

4. **Organize evidence and data gathered through interviews and other information sources by using 3x5 cards to record information from each source.**

   What did I find out from each source?

   Which of my questions have been answered by which sources?

   What are some ideas which I found in more than one source?

   What are some issues about which my sources disagreed?

5. **Prepare a report based on your ordered cards. Remember to answer all of the following questions in your report.**

   What is the issue or problem?

   What different perspectives are taken on the issue?

   What is your position?

   What data or evidence support your position?

   What conclusions do you make about your issue?

   What consequences do you see of your position?

6. **Communicate your findings. (Prepare an oral presentation for classmates based on notecards and written report.)**

   What are my purpose, issue, and point of view, and how will I explain them?

   What data will I use to support my point of view?

   How will I conclude my presentation?

Topic Web

(Handout 10F)

NAME: _____ DATE: _____

What do I want to
know?
(List questions.)

What information
resources would be best
to pursue for each
question? (books,
periodicals, people,
Internet, CD-ROM)

TOPIC

What did I find out from
each source?

What did I learn?

LESSON

11

Understanding Poetry

CURRICULUM ALIGNMENT CODE

GOAL 1	GOAL 2	GOAL 3	GOAL 4	GOAL 5	GOAL 6
X	X		X		X

INSTRUCTIONAL PURPOSE

- ▼ To develop interpretation skills in literature by discussing poetry.
- ▼ To explore the concept of change in a personal context.
- ▼ To develop persuasive writing skills.

MATERIALS USED

1. Copies of "poem for rodney," "Poem," and "Perfection"
2. Student **Response Journals**
3. Change Matrix (Handout 3B from Lesson 3)
4. Photographs of students (requested in Lesson 10)
5. Writing about Change Assignment (Handout 11A)

ACTIVITIES

1. Begin the lesson by reading (silently and aloud) *poem for rodney, Poem*, and *Perfection*. Briefly discuss each poem, using the questions below as a guide.

"poem for rodney"—Nikki Giovanni

- ▼ *State an important idea from the poem.*
- ▼ *What does the author mean by "i always just think i'd like to grow up"?*
- ▼ *Why do you think the poet uses the small "i" to talk about herself?*

▼ *Why do you think the author chose this title? What might be another title for this poem? What parts of the poem gave you the idea for your title?*

"Perfection"—Felice Holman

▼ *What is the main idea of the poem? Why is it called "Perfection"?*

▼ *The author sees flaws, or something wrong, in the turkey and the hog. What are they? What flaw does she see in the goose?*

▼ *What does the author think about trading places with the "odd-necked goose"? Why might the goose want or not want to trade with the author? Why might the author want or not want to trade with the goose?*

▼ *What does the author seem to be saying about the concept of "perfection"? What does it mean to be perfect?*

▼ *How do our ideas about change apply to this poem?*

"Poem"—Langston Hughes

▼ *Why does the poet use the word "soft" in line 5? What does the word "soft" mean in this poem?*

▼ *What can happen when a friend leaves your life? What are the effects for you? What are the effects for your friend? What feelings might you both have?*

▼ *In what ways could this kind of change happen in a person's life? How do our generalizations about change fit the situation in the poem?*

▼ *What causes friendships to end?*

▼ *This piece is titled simply "Poem." What might be another title for this poem? What are your reasons for choosing your title?*

2. Ask students to write in their **Response Journals** about their feelings for a friend and how they would feel if that friend went away.

3. As a whole class activity, complete the column of the **Change Matrix** (Handout 3B) that applies to this reading. Have students complete their notebook copy of the Matrix as well as filling in the butcher paper or posterboard copy. The completed grid will serve as the basis for a discussion in a later lesson about change.

4. Lead a discussion on the characteristics of **Poetic Writing**. In what way does it differ from story writing? In what ways is it similar? As a class, make a Venn diagram comparing poetic writing and story writing.

5. Encourage students to think of ideas for poetry writing and how they may express some different ideas and feelings in their poetry than they do in their prose writing. Brainstorm some ideas for poetry and include them as prompts for writing in the Writing/Computer Center.

6. Students were asked to bring two pictures of themselves to class (Homework from Lesson 10). Ask students to look carefully at the two pictures and to think of the many different ways **they have changed**. Give each student a long sheet of paper (e.g., 8½" x 14"). Have them divide the paper into four sections by folding it in half lengthwise and across. Students should then glue or tape the younger picture of themselves at the top and the older one at the center of the sheet where the folds cross. Of the two sections between the photos, students may label one "Changes" and one "No changes," and then fill in the two sections with ideas on how they have and have not changed since they were younger. Encourage them to think beyond physical changes, considering their likes and dislikes, their abilities, and their ideas as well as their appearance.

   At the bottom of their sheet of paper, have students draw a picture of what they think they will be like when they grow up (or reach high school, etc.). Have them fill in the sections between their present and future pictures with changes they expect to see in themselves and the things they do not expect to change about themselves.

   Allow students to share their projects with one another, encouraging them to ask questions about how the past and intended changes fit with the class generalizations about change. (Example: Which of these changes will you cause to happen? Which will happen naturally? Which of the changes you have seen in yourself have been positive? Which have been negative? etc.) After the discussion, display student papers in the classroom.

7. Review any of the generalizations about change that did not arise in the previous discussion. Distribute copies of the **Writing about Change** assignment (Handout 11A) and discuss with students. Each student should select *one* of the change generalizations and brainstorm ideas of how it has been true in his or her own life. Review the parts of a persuasive paragraph, using the Hamburger Model. Students should then select at least three good ideas from their list and draft a persuasive paragraph. This activity may be started in class and completed for homework, so that students will have a draft available for revision in the next lesson.

NOTE TO TEACHER

The activity students completed in this lesson to show changes in themselves may be added as an option at the Reading Center for showing changes in characters. Students may draw pictures of a character at the top and bottom of a paper, representing the character at the beginning and at the end of the story, and then indicate what changed and did not change about the character throughout the story.

HOMEWORK

Complete a draft of your Writing about Change assignment.

EXTENSIONS

1. Read poems by the following authors: Shel Silverstein, Emily Dickinson, and Robert Frost.

2. Choose one of your poems, select two words you think are interesting and explain why you chose them.

3. Begin a poetry journal, in which you write your own poems about topics of your choosing. You may choose to publish and illustrate your poems at the Writing Center.

4. Make a collection of objects that represent change. They might be signs of change in nature, things that help changes to occur, or reminders of changes in your own life. Design a project with your objects. You may make a collage, write a poem or essay about your objects, or do another project of your choosing.

Writing about Change

(Handout 11A)

NAME: _____ DATE: _____

We have discussed how the five generalizations about change are true in the world around us and in the literature we have read. Now think about how the generalizations have been true in your own life. Select one of the generalizations and write it below. Then list examples from your own life of how the generalization has been true for you.

Generalization:

Examples:

   Write a persuasive paragraph arguing that the generalization you selected is true, based on your own experiences. State your opinion on the issue, then give at least three reasons which show evidence that the generalization is true. Explain your reasons thoroughly. Write a conclusion to end your paragraph.

LESSON

12

▼

Writing Poetry

CURRICULUM ALIGNMENT CODE

GOAL 1	GOAL 2	GOAL 3	GOAL 4	GOAL 5	GOAL 6
X		X			X

INSTRUCTIONAL PURPOSE

▼ To enhance linguistic competency by using the poetic form diamante.

▼ To explore the concept of change through the writing of diamante poems.

▼ To develop revision skills in student writing.

▼ To develop analytical and interpretive skills in literature.

MATERIALS USED

1. Diamante poem examples ("Ice" and "Anger") (Handout 12A)
2. Completed Writing Assignments (from Lesson 11)
3. Self-Assessment for Writing (Handout 12B)
4. Peer Assessment for Writing (Handout 12C)
5. Teacher Assessment for Writing (Handout 12D)
6. Poetry selections from *Hailstones and Halibut Bones** (for lesson extension)

ACTIVITIES

1. Explain that students will use the poetic form of a diamante to create their own poems about change. Share with the class the two poems "Ice" and "Anger" on Handout 12A.

*O'Neill, M. (1989). *Hailstones and halibut bones.* New York: Doubleday.

131

2. Use the following questions in the discussion:

- ▼ *Where do you see change happening in the poems?*
- ▼ *What is an antonym?*
- ▼ *What part of speech are the words in the second line? Third line?*
- ▼ *What is special about the phrases in line four?*
- ▼ *How does the form of the poem change as the poem is developed? What does it look like, and how does it sound?*
- ▼ *How does the number of words per line change as the poem is developed? What is the effect of the changes?*
- ▼ *What might make some diamante poems more interesting or more appealing than others? (how well it adheres to the form, use of expressive language, visual and auditory appeal, etc.)*

3. Guide the class in identifying, line by line, the parts of speech of selected words. Make sure students know what is meant by nouns and adjectives. Discuss the effects of different types of words in the process of creating images through poetry.

4. On a transparency, present the diamante poetic form and discuss how it applies to "Ice."

5. Have students generate some pairs of words which might be the top and bottom words of a diamante. Select one of the pairs and use it to write a class diamante. Discuss different ways of developing such a poem, including writing it from the top down or from the two selected nouns toward the center.

6. Have students work in pairs to create diamante poems. Share the poems and discuss how they show change from one end to the other.

7. Encourage students to generate a list of paired antonyms which demonstrate the idea that change is linked to time. (Example: night/day, summer/winter.) Tell them to select one of the pairs to use in a diamante poem they will write for homework.

8. Have students work in small groups to share the persuasive paragraphs they wrote about changes in their own lives (Lesson 11). Distribute copies of the **Self-Assessment** and **Peer Assessment for Writing** (Handouts 12B and 12C) and encourage students to use them to guide discussion and suggestions for revision. Students may also confer with the teacher on their writing. Provide time for revising based on peer and teacher comments.

HOMEWORK

1. Write a diamante poem based on the pair of words you chose from the list about changes linked to time.

2. Revise your persuasive paragraph based on comments from your peers and the teacher.

EXTENSIONS

1. Read some poems from an anthology of children's poetry. Select a favorite poem and give three reasons why it is your favorite.

2. Diamante poems can also be written with antonyms that are not nouns. Think of two adjectives which are opposites (happy/sad, bright/dark) and write a diamante about them.

3. Read color poems from *Hailstones and Halibut Bones*. Make up a diamante poem about two colors.

Diamante Poem
(Handout 12A)

NAME: _____ DATE: _____

topic (noun)

two describing words (adjectives)

three action words (verbs or "ing" action words)

a four-word phrase capturing some feeling about the topic

three action words (verbs or "ing" words)

two describing words (adjectives)

ending word (noun, antonym for topic)

Examples

Anger	**Ice**
anger	ice
boiling, red-faced	smooth, solid
shouting, crying, pacing	gliding, skating, slipping
can't believe this happened	winter fun for skaters
talking, listening, talking	thawing, cracking, melting
calmer, quiet	thin, unsafe
acceptance	water

Self-Assessment for Writing

(Handout 12B)

NAME: _____ DATE: _____

ASSIGNMENT: _____

Directions: Grade your own writing. For each sentence below, circle the choice that describes your writing best.

1. My main idea is clear.	Needs Improvement	Satisfactory	Excellent
2. My details support the main idea.	Needs Improvement	Satisfactory	Excellent
3. My ideas flow smoothly and orderly.	Needs Improvement	Satisfactory	Excellent
4. The hamburger paragraph structure is clear (introduction, body, conclusion).	Needs Improvement	Satisfactory	Excellent
5. My vocabulary is rich and varied.	Needs Improvement	Satisfactory	Excellent

MY WRITING IS STRONG IN THESE WAYS:

_____

_____

_____

MY WRITING COULD BE IMPROVED IN THESE WAYS:

_____

_____

_____

Peer Assessment for Writing
(Handout 12C)

READER: _____ WRITER: _____

ASSIGNMENT: _____

Directions: Read your partner's writing sample carefully. For each sentence below, circle the choice that you think describes the writing.

1. The main idea is clear.	Needs Improvement	Satisfactory	Excellent
2. The details support the main idea.	Needs Improvement	Satisfactory	Excellent
3. The ideas flow smoothly and orderly.	Needs Improvement	Satisfactory	Excellent
4. The hamburger paragraph structure is clear (introduction, body, conclusion).	Needs Improvement	Satisfactory	Excellent
5. The vocabulary is rich and varied.	Needs Improvement	Satisfactory	Excellent

THE WRITING SAMPLE IS STRONG IN THESE WAYS:

_____

_____

_____

THE WRITING SAMPLE COULD BE IMPROVED IN THESE WAYS:

_____

_____

_____

Teacher Assessment for Writing
(Handout 12D)

STUDENT: _____ DATE: _____

ASSIGNMENT: _____

Directions: Circle the words that best describe the writing.

1. The main idea is clear.	Needs Improvement	Satisfactory	Excellent
2. Appropriate level of detail is provided to support the main idea.	Needs Improvement	Satisfactory	Excellent
3. The ideas flow smoothly and orderly.	Needs Improvement	Satisfactory	Excellent
4. The hamburger paragraph structure is clear (introduction, body, conclusion).	Needs Improvement	Satisfactory	Excellent
5. The writing uses descriptive language and rich vocabulary.	Needs Improvement	Satisfactory	Excellent
Optional: Demonstrates correct grammar, usage, and mechanics.	Needs Improvement	Satisfactory	Excellent

PARTICULAR STRENGTHS:

_____

_____

AREAS NEEDING IMPROVEMENT:

_____

_____

LESSON

13

▼

Exploring Change through Art

CURRICULUM ALIGNMENT CODE

GOAL 1	GOAL 2	GOAL 3	GOAL 4	GOAL 5	GOAL 6
	X				X

INSTRUCTIONAL PURPOSE

▼ To expand the concept of change through interdisciplinary study of Escher art.

▼ To use symmetry and tessellations to create an image of change.

▼ To link art and literature through the works of Escher and Wiesner.

▼ To develop editing skills in student writing.

MATERIALS USED

1. *The Graphic Work of M. C. Escher* by M. C. Escher*

2. Student **Response Journals**

3. Creating Tessellations with Pattern Blocks (Handout 13A)

4. Pattern blocks (Available from Dale Seymour or Creative Publications)

5. *Free Fall* by David Wiesner**

6. Change Model (Handout 13B)

7. Completed Writing about Change Assignment (from Lesson 11)

*Escher, M. C. (1967). *The graphic work of M. C. Escher* (rev. ed.). New York: Ballantine.

**Wiesner, D. (1988). *Free fall*. New York: Lothrop, Lee & Shepard.

TESSELLATIONS RESOURCES FOR TEACHERS

Available from Dale Seymour Publications, P. O. Box 10888, Palo Alto, CA 94303-0879 or (800) 872-1100 or FAX (415) 324-3424:

▼ *Introductions to Tessellation,* by Dale Seymour and Jill Britton

▼ *Teaching Tessellating Art,* by Jill Britton and Walter Britton

Available from Creative Publications, 5005 West 110th Street, Oaklawn, IL 60453 or (800) 624-0822 or in Illinois (800) 435-5843:

▼ *Creating Escher-Type Drawings,* by E. R. Ranucci and J. L. Teeters

▼ *Tessellations: The Geometry of Patterns,* by S. Bezuska, M. Kenney, and L. Silvey.

ACTIVITIES

1. Distribute individual copies or display a poster of M. C. Escher's *Night and Day.* (This woodcut features images of white and black birds flying over fields, towns, and rivers. Symmetry and tessellations are used in unique ways to create a remarkable effect.)

2. Have students write in their **Response Journals** an answer to the following question, then share in small groups:

    What do you see in the picture?

3. As a whole class activity, discuss the picture, focusing on these questions:

    ▼ *How is this picture similar to a diamante poem?*

    ▼ *The "mirror images" demonstrate* **symmetry.** *What is symmetry? How does symmetry contribute to the effect of the picture?*

    ▼ *The artist called this woodcut* Night and Day. *Create another title for it and give two reasons for your title.*

    ▼ *What does this picture tell us about change? Which of the generalizations about change can apply?*

4. Have students write diamante poems with the words "night" and "day," based on the Escher picture. These poems may be shared in pairs and revised, then published and posted around the Escher print.

5. Introduce the concept of a tessellation. Show students that a tessellation is a design created by repeating a pattern with no spaces between the shapes. Explain that a tessellation can be created by repeating one shape many times; for example, point out repeating tiles on a linoleum floor or ceiling tiles which

repeat the same shape. Give students pattern blocks and the **Tessellation Activity** (Handout 13A). Ask them to determine with the pattern blocks which of the shapes on the sheet can be used to create a tessellation. Discuss the results on the investigation.

6. Continuing the exploration of tessellations, have students use pattern blocks to create tessellations with two or more shapes. Invite them to share their tessellations in small groups. Have students copy their tessellations onto paper and color them so that the patterns may be preserved. (A second option would be for students to glue construction paper shapes onto another sheet in the patterns of their tessellations.) Display student work in the classroom.

7. Return to Escher's *Night and Day*, and ask students to find examples of tessellations in the picture. Discuss the effects created by the use of the tessellations. Show and discuss other examples of Escher's prints, especially *Metamorphose*, and compare to *Night and Day*.

    ▼ *What examples of symmetry do you see? What do they contribute to the artwork?*

    ▼ *Where are tessellations used? How do they affect the quality of the artwork?*

    ▼ *What do these works illustrate about change?*

8. Invite students to explore the book, *Free Fall*, by David Wiesner. In this wordless picture book, a boy's dream transforms ordinary objects into an adventure. Wiesner uses ideas and images that are similar to Escher's work. Discuss the book, using the following questions.

    ▼ *How are the images in* Free Fall *similar to Escher's* Night and Day *and* Metamorphose?

    ▼ *Where do you see tessellations used in* Free Fall?

    ▼ *How do our generalizations about change apply to* Free Fall? *What kinds of changes do you see occurring in the book? What causes the changes?*

9. Divide students into small groups. Assign each group three consecutive panels of the story to examine, listing and discussing the specific changes they see occurring. Ask the groups to title each of their three panels and be prepared to give reasons for their titles. Distribute copies of the **Change Model** (Handout 13B). Have students continue working in their groups to complete the model with ideas from

Free Fall. As a class, discuss titles given to specific panels and responses to the Change Model.

10. Introduce the last Learning Center for the unit:

    ### Art/Writing Center

    This Center should contain a number of art cards which display prints of various artworks, including some of Escher's works. Students may use these cards as prompts for poetry or story writing or to answer questions about change (which may include completing a change model or answering specific questions listed on the art cards).

11. Provide time for students to work in pairs to read one another's Writing about Change paragraphs (from Lesson 11) for editing purposes. Students may also consult with the teacher on questions related to editing. Students should then write a final copy of their work to be displayed in the classroom or put into a class book.

NOTE TO TEACHER

The pictures in Free Fall *were created end to end as one continuous mural. Encourage students to note the continuity of the pictures in order to observe change from the beginning to the end of the book. Two copies of the book may be pulled apart and reconnected as a long, continuous mural to demonstrate the effect.*

HOMEWORK

1. Complete final copy of change paragraph.

2. Complete *one* of the following two assignments:

    a. Write a diamante poem about two parts of *Free Fall.*

    b. Think of one of your favorite stories. Imagine that the boy in *Free Fall* dreamed he was in that story, and draw what might have happened. For an extra challenge, draw his movement from one of your favorite stories to another.

EXTENSIONS

1. Examine other works by Escher and other "pattern" artists like Vaserely and Mondrian. How are their works alike and different?

2. The pictures in *Free Fall* relate to other well-known works of literature. (*Alice in Wonderland* and *Gulliver's Travels,* for example.) Explore these other works of literature and discuss how they influenced *Free Fall.*

3. Write a story to go with *Free Fall.* Give titles to each of the pictures.

Creating Tessellations with Pattern Blocks

(Handout 13A)

NAME: _____ DATE: _____

Shape	Can you create a tessellation with this shape?

Change Model
(Handout 13B)

NAME: _____ DATE: _____

Develop a list of three–five examples for each of the following statements (generalizations) about change.

Change is linked to time:

Change is everywhere:

Change

Change may be positive:

. . . or negative:

Change may be perceived as orderly:

. . . or random:

Change may happen naturally:

or may be caused by people:

LESSON

14

Oral Communication

CURRICULUM ALIGNMENT CODE

GOAL 1	GOAL 2	GOAL 3	GOAL 4	GOAL 5	GOAL 6
			X	X	

INSTRUCTIONAL PURPOSE

▼ To introduce listening and oral communication skills.

▼ To develop reasoning skills.

MATERIALS USED

1. *Free Fall*

2. 3x5 index cards

3. Assorted wordless picture books

4. Oral Presentation Evaluation Form (Handout 14A)

ACTIVITIES

1. Give each student four 3x5 index cards. Ask them to write the following headings, one on each card: **purpose, sequence of events, ending,** and **main idea**.

2. Recall students' attention to Wiesner's *Free Fall*, discussed in Lesson 13. On the board or overhead, invite student contributions to develop responses for each of the headings based on the book. Then give a brief oral presentation based on the responses, demonstrating for students how to organize information and speak from notes.

3. Distribute wordless picture books to the class, one to each student. Have students study the books, then respond on the index cards to the following four headings, describing the author's **purpose, 3–5 events in sequence**, the **ending of the story**, and the **main idea** or **message** of the story. Circulate and assist students in the presentation development process.

4. Encourage students to work with a partner to practice their oral presentations.

5. Distribute and discuss the **Oral Presentation Evaluation Form** (Handout 14A). Have students take turns standing and presenting the information about their books based on the responses on the cards. Encourage students to use the evaluation form to comment on one another's presentations.

6. Discuss the presentations in small groups, encouraging students to comment on the organization of one another's presentations.

7. The teacher may also wish to discuss issues of oral communication such as consideration of audience, purpose, and nature of message.

NOTE TO TEACHER

The main emphasis in this lesson should be on the organization and content of oral presentations, more so than issues such as eye contact and voice level in presentation. Although these issues should be emphasized for oral presentations, the primary purpose here is to introduce students to the organizational process.

HOMEWORK

Watch a television program of no longer than 30 minutes. Write the purpose, sequence, ending, and message on notecards. Bring to class tomorrow, prepared to give an oral presentation.

Oral Presentation Evaluation Form

(Handout 14A)

NAME: _____ DATE: _____

ASSIGNMENT: _____

Directions: Circle the choice that describes each of the following best.

ORGANIZATION

1. The purpose of the presentation was clear.   Needs Improvement   Satisfactory   Excellent

2. The speaker included good examples.   Needs Improvement   Satisfactory   Excellent

3. The speaker showed knowledge of the subject.   Needs Improvement   Satisfactory   Excellent

4. The presentation closed with a strong, interesting idea that restated the purpose.   Needs Improvement   Satisfactory   Excellent

DELIVERY

1. The speaker made good eye contact with the audience.   Needs Improvement   Satisfactory   Excellent

2. The presentation was loud enough.   Needs Improvement   Satisfactory   Excellent

3. The speaker's words were clear enough to be understood.   Needs Improvement   Satisfactory   Excellent

THE BEST PART OF THIS PRESENTATION WAS:

_____

_____

A SUGGESTION FOR IMPROVEMENT IS:

_____

_____

LESSON
15
Inside and Outside Changes

CURRICULUM ALIGNMENT CODE

GOAL 1	GOAL 2	GOAL 3	GOAL 4	GOAL 5	GOAL 6
X	X	X		X	X

INSTRUCTIONAL PURPOSE

▼ To develop reasoning and interpretive skills in literature through discussing "The Ugly Duckling."

▼ To explore new vocabulary words.

MATERIALS USED

1. Hand mirrors

2. "The Ugly Duckling" by Hans Christian Andersen

3. Literature Web—Primary Adaptation (Handout 15A)

4. Student **Response Journals**

5. Vocabulary Web (Handout 15B)

6. Change Matrix (Handout 3B, from Lesson 3)

ACTIVITIES

1. Open the lesson by distributing hand mirrors to each student. Direct students to look into the mirror and to think of two changes they would like to make about themselves and two things they would not change. Guide a discussion of students' reflections, considering the idea that how you look is not as important as what type of person you are.

2. Ask students to think of a time when they or someone they knew had problems because of the way that they looked. Explain that the story for this session,

"The Ugly Duckling" by Hans Christian Andersen, is about an animal who had problems because of how he looked.

3. Distribute copies of "The Ugly Duckling" to each student to be read silently.

4. Have students work in groups to do a **Literature Web** (Handout 15A) for "The Ugly Duckling."

5. After students have read the story, conduct a discussion based on the following questions.

Literary Response and Interpretation Questions

▼ *What is the "problem" with the duckling in the story?*

▼ *How was the way the cat and the hen treated the duckling different from how the other animals treated him?*

▼ *What do you think is the main idea of the story?*

▼ *Do you agree with the hen's description of how to recognize a true friend? Why or why not?*

▼ *"A good heart never becomes proud." What might that sentence mean? Can you give examples other than from the story to illustrate the meaning?*

Reasoning Questions

▼ *What reasons are given by the other animals for rejecting the duckling?*

▼ *What evidence is there in the story that even the duckling's mother rejects him?*

▼ *How does the idea of "the pain of being different" relate to this story?*

Change Questions

▼ *How does the idea of change apply to this story? How do our five generalizations fit with the story?*

6. Have students find the word "pride" in the dictionary, then work in groups to create a concept map about pride. Have them consider when it might be considered good to feel proud and when it might be considered bad to feel proud.

7. Have students write in their **Response Journal** about the following question:

   ▼ *Write about an experience when you felt "the pain of being different."*

8. Have students work in groups to complete a **Vocabulary Web** (Handout 15B) for one of the following words from "The Ugly Duckling": *scoundrel, admonished, aristocratic, mocked, probation, and persecuted*.

9. As a whole class activity, complete the column of the **Change Matrix** (Handout 3B) that applies to this reading. Have students complete their notebook copy of the Matrix as well as filling in the butcher paper or posterboard copy. The completed grid will serve as the basis for a discussion in later lessons about change.

HOMEWORK

Complete *one* of the following two homework assignments:

1. What does beauty mean to you? Create a collage of the three most beautiful things in your life. Describe in a page why each is beautiful to you.

2. Write two diamante poems about "The Ugly Duckling," one to describe changes on the outside of a character and one to describe changes on the inside of a character.

EXTENSIONS

1. Hans Christian Andersen's stories have inspired numerous illustrators and translators. You may enjoy comparing the work of different illustrators or comparing some of Andersen's stories that are new to you. Illustrated versions of single stories and collections of Andersen's stories are often in different places in a library. Ask a librarian to help you find them. Some examples are listed below:

Andersen, H. C. (1959). *Seven tales by Hans Christian Andersen* (E. LeGallienne, Trans.). New York: Harper & Row.

Andersen, H. C. (1965). *The nightingale* (E. LeGallienne, Trans.). New York: Harper & Row.

Andersen, H. C. (1978). *Hans Andersen: His classic fairy tales* (E. Haugaard, Trans.). New York: Doubleday.

Andersen, H. C. (1981). *The wild swans* (A. Ehrlich, Retold). New York: Dial.

Andersen, H. C. (1985). *The nightingale* (A. Bell, Trans.). New York: Picture Book Studio.

Andersen, H. C. (1985). *The nightingale* (A. Bier, Adapted). New York: Harcourt Brace Jovanovich.

JOURNEYS
AND
DESTINATIONS

Literature Web—
Primary Adaptation
(Handout 15A)

NAME: _____ DATE: _____

Key Words

Feelings

Reading

Ideas

Images or
Symbols

Vocabulary Web
(Handout 15B)

NAME: _____ DATE: _____

Synonyms:

Sentence:

Definition:

Antonyms:

Word:

Part of Speech:

Example:

Analysis

Word Families:

Stems:

Origin:

LESSON

16

An Author and His Work

CURRICULUM ALIGNMENT CODE					
GOAL 1	GOAL 2	GOAL 3	GOAL 4	GOAL 5	GOAL 6
X				X	X

INSTRUCTIONAL PURPOSE

▼ To discuss change in the life of an author (Hans Christian Andersen) as well as in the character of his story ("The Ugly Duckling").

▼ To explore interdisciplinary connections among fields by discussing biographies.

▼ To develop understanding of the concept of change.

MATERIALS USED

1. Biographical Sketch of Hans Christian Andersen (Handout 16A)

2. *Mathematicians Are People, Too**

3. Selected biographies of artists, authors, scientists

ACTIVITIES

1. Ask students to think about how they get ideas for writing. As a class, brainstorm about how different authors may get writing ideas. Explain that this activity will focus on how the life of **Hans Christian Andersen**, author of "The Ugly Duckling," was similar to the life of the duckling.

2. Have students read the **Biographical Sketch** of Hans Christian Andersen (Handout 16A). Encourage them to look as they read for ways the author's life is similar to and different from his story, "The Ugly Duckling." Allow approximately 30 minutes for students to read the biographical sketch and work in small groups to

*Reimer, L., & Reimer, W. (1990). *Mathematicians are people, too*. Palo Alto, CA: Dale Seymour.

create a Venn diagram comparing the author's life and his story. Monitor and assist students as they work, then discuss as a class and make a large-group Venn diagram.

3. Discuss how to find out about a person's life and the changes that person may have undergone. Have students work in groups to write five questions they might ask an adult to find out about changes in that person's life. Compile a class list of questions, from which each student should select five to use in interviewing his or her parents about change.

4. From the book *Mathematicians Are People, Too,* read the sketch of Isaac Newton's life. Discuss with students how Newton was like Hans Christian Andersen and how the two men were different. Use the following questions as a guide.

   ▼ *What was Isaac Newton's life like when he was growing up? How was he like Hans Christian Andersen when he was young?*

   ▼ *Isaac Newton once said, "If I have seen farther than others, it is because I have stood on the shoulders of giants." What does this quote mean? Why did Isaac Newton feel special to have "seen farther than others"?*

   ▼ *Both of the people we have read about found a special talent in themselves. What were their special talents? What are some other special talents people might have?*

5. Have students work in pairs to read a short biography or biographical sketch of a famous individual in the arts or sciences. Have each pair create a chart about their person similar to the change charts students completed about themselves (Lesson 11). In one column of the chart, students should record changes in the person's life; in the other column, they should record things that did not change. After completing the chart, students should write a paragraph explaining how particular changes and events in the person's life helped them to decide on the career he or she chose. Invite each pair to share their paragraph and change chart with another pair.

HOMEWORK

Use the questions you wrote in class to interview your parents about major changes in their lives. Write a one-page paper telling about them.

EXTENSION

Read another story about being different. Choose from the following list.

Cooney, B. (1982). *Miss Rumphius*. New York: Viking.

Jarrell, R. (1963). *The bat-poet*. New York: Macmillan.

Pinkwater, D. M. (1977). *The big orange splot*. New York: Hastings.

Tolan, S. (1983). *A time to fly free*. New York: Scribner.

Create a poster showing how the main character changed throughout the story. Compare the character to the Ugly Duckling. Make a list of the ways they are alike and different.

Biographical Sketch of Hans Christian Andersen

(Handout 16A)

NAME: _____ DATE: _____

Hans Christian Anderson is famous for writing many enchanting fairy tales, including "The Ugly Duckling" and "The Emperor's New Clothes." He was born in 1805 in Odense, on the island of Fyn, in Denmark. He was the only child in a poor family. His father, a cobbler, died when he was 11, and his mother took a job as a washer woman, leaving Hans to dream and fantasize alone.

In school, the other children made fun of Andersen's awkwardness and his large hands and feet. After his father's death, he stopped going to school. Instead, he stayed at home, reading as many books as he could find and creating puppets and paper cut-outs. His own make-believe games, combined with the fantastic stories his mother told him as a child, laid the foundation for the fairy tales he wrote as an adult.

At the age of 14, Andersen left home for Copenhagen in hopes of becoming an opera singer and dancer. Because of his poor voice and lanky, awkward body his musical dream was never fulfilled. However, he met several friends who encouraged his writing and education and eventually made it possible for him to go to a university. He did not like the university, where he studied for six years. Even though he towered over the younger students, both the students and teachers bullied him.

As an adult, Andersen earned his living by writing. In 1829 he wrote his first successful book. It earned him enough money to travel around Europe. He then wrote about his travels in a novel. In 1835 he published a book of fairy tales. He continued to write novels, plays, and travel sketches, but he also began a second and third series of fairy tales. His stories were translated into English, and Andersen became a celebrity wherever he traveled. Children accepted and loved him, and they understood him better than grownups. Andersen never married. He continued to write fairy tales until he died in 1875 at the age of 70. During his lifetime he wrote 168 fairy tales.

17

Bringing the Rain to Kapiti Plain

CURRICULUM ALIGNMENT CODE

GOAL 1	GOAL 2	GOAL 3	GOAL 4	GOAL 5	GOAL 6
X		X		X	X

INSTRUCTIONAL PURPOSE

▼ To develop reasoning about literature through discussion of the African folk tale *Bringing the Rain to Kapiti Plain*.

▼ To explore new vocabulary words.

▼ To explore interdisciplinary and real-world connections with science and social studies.

MATERIALS USED

1. Globe and individual maps of Africa

2. *Bringing the Rain to Kapiti Plain* by Verna Aardema*

3. Literature Web—Primary Adaptation (Handout 17A)

4. Vocabulary Web (Handout 17B)

5. *Rain Player* by D. Wisniewski**

6. Student **Response Journals**

7. Change Matrix (Handout 3B, from Lesson 3)

ACTIVITIES

1. Use a globe and maps to locate the country of Kenya in Africa. Explain that the story to be read in this lesson is a folk tale from Kenya. Ask students to contribute what they know about this part of the world and about life there to a discussion.

*Aardema, V. (1981). *Bringing the rain to Kapiti plain*. NY: The Dial Press.
**Wisniewski, D. (1991) *Rain Player*. New York: Clarion.

2. Read *Bringing the Rain to Kapiti Plain* aloud as a class.

3. Have students work in groups to do a **Literature Web** (Handout 17A) for *Bringing the Rain to Kapiti Plain*. At this point, teachers may choose to introduce the **Structure** piece of the Literature Web, as this story lends itself well to a discussion of structure (see Literature Web discussion in Section III). Ask students to what nursery rhyme this book is similar. Read a version of "The House that Jack Built" and compare the two to enhance the discussion of structure.

4. Guide a discussion based on the following questions.

Literary Response and Interpretation Questions

▼ *What caused the grass to turn brown?*

▼ *What are some of the other things that happened as a result of no rain?*

▼ *What did Ki-pat do to solve the problem of no rain?*

▼ *What important qualities did Ki-pat have?*

▼ *Why did Ki-pat think of using a feather?*

▼ *How does this story show the relationship of cause and effect in nature?*

▼ *Why did the author end the story with Ki-pat's son tending the herds?*

▼ *How might the story have been different if the cows had died?*

▼ *In your opinion, what is the best part of the story? Why?*

Change Questions

▼ *How are the five generalizations about change brought out in this folk tale?*

▼ *Was the major change in this story caused by humans or by nature?*

5. Have students write in their **Response Journal** about one of the following questions:

▼ *The drought in Africa was a terrible problem for Ki-pat in the story. It also is a terrible problem in the world today, along with famine. Write a paragraph arguing why our country should provide help to parts of the world suffering from famine and drought. You may write your argument in the form of a letter to the President or to the editor of a newspaper.* (**Note to Teacher:** *This activity provides an opportunity to introduce UNICEF and other world help organizations here.*)

▼ *Think about hero stories in different cultures. How is Superman different from Ki-pat? How are they alike?*

6. As a whole class activity, complete a **Vocabulary Web** (Handout 17B) for the following word from the story, *Bringing the Rain to Kapiti Plain*: **migrated**.

7. As a whole class activity, complete the column of the **Change Matrix** (Handout 3B) that applies to this reading. Have students complete their copy of the Matrix as well as filling in the butcher paper or posterboard copy. The completed grid will serve as the basis for a discussion in a later lesson about change.

8. Read *Rain Player* by David Wisniewski. As a class, discuss briefly how the book is similar to and different from *Bringing the Rain to Kapiti Plain*. Have students create individual Venn diagrams comparing the two stories.

HOMEWORK

Use your Venn diagram about *Rain Player* and *Bringing the Rain to Kapiti Plain* to write a two-paragraph paper. One paragraph should describe how the stories are alike, and the other should explain how they are different.

EXTENSIONS

1. How widespread is drought and famine in Africa? Research causes and effects of these problems. Prepare a chart or graph to show how Africa as a continent is affected.

2. Find out about drought in other areas of the world and in other times in history. When has drought caused a major problem in this country? (**Note to Teacher:** Opportunity to discuss the Dust Bowl crisis of the Great Depression; the photographic work of Dorothea Lange provides a resource.)

3. **Note to Teacher:** A discussion of drought leads clearly to interdisciplinary connections with science and social studies, as indicated in the two extensions above. In addition, teachers may wish to investigate the Center for Gifted Education's problem-based science unit *Dust Bowl* to extend this discussion further. [Available from Kendall/Hunt; call 1-800-228-0810.]

4. **Note to Teacher:** Extend the discussion of heroes (see **Response Journal** question, on page 170) with a comparison of *technology-based cultures* and *earth-based cultures* (from Chellis Glendinning, *When Technology Wounds*). Discuss how such societies differ and how their heroes and stories differ as a consequence.

5. If you enjoyed reading *Bringing the Rain to Kapiti Plain*, you may enjoy reading these other books by Verna Aardema:

   Aardema, V. (1985). *Bimiwili and the Zimwi*. New York: Dial.

   Aardema, V. (1984). *Oh, Kojo! How could you!* New York: Dial.

   Aardema, V. (1960). *What's so funny, Ketu? A Nuer tale*. New York: Dial.

   Aardema, V. (1984). *Who's in Rabbit's house?* New York: Dial.

   Aardema, V. (1984). *Why mosquitoes buzz in people's ears*. New York: Dial.

Think about some common characteristics of her books. Describe three characteristics and give examples from the books to support your description.

Literature Web—
Primary Adaptation
(Handout 17A)

NAME: _____ DATE: _____

Key Words

Feelings

Reading

Ideas

Images or Symbols

Vocabulary Web

(Handout 17B)

NAME: _____ DATE: _____

Synonyms:

Sentence:

Definition:

Antonyms:

Word:

Part of Speech:

Example:

Analysis

Word Families:

Stems:

Origin:

LESSON

18

Writing from Research

CURRICULUM ALIGNMENT CODE

GOAL 1	GOAL 2	GOAL 3	GOAL 4	GOAL 5	GOAL 6
	X			X	

INSTRUCTIONAL PURPOSE

▼ To develop writing skills through a short paper that supports a point of view on the best ways to remember.

▼ To develop reasoning skills through persuasive writing.

MATERIALS USED

1. Student research materials and notes from Lesson 10, *Remembering and Research*

2. Self-Assessment for Writing (Handout 18A)

3. Peer Assessment for Writing (Handout 18B)

4. Teacher Assessment for Writing (Handout 18C)

5. Standards for Reasoning (Handout 18D)

ACTIVITIES

1. Students should bring to class all their information and notes about their **Research Issue**, the assignment from Lesson 10 involving investigating the best ways to preserve memories.

2. Return to the **Topic Web** from Lesson 10 (Handout 10F). Review the issue and encourage students to refer to their own Topic Webs to share what they have learned from various sources and what might be some answers to their questions.

3. Review the stages of the writing process and the parts of the Hamburger Model with students (Lesson 5). Encourage students to begin drafting a persuasive paper answering the question, "What is the best way to preserve memories?" The paper should state the student's point of view on the issue, give several reasons with elaboration to support the point of view, and provide a conclusion.

4. Have students work in pairs to share their papers and offer comments. Encourage them to use the **Self-Assessment** and **Peer Assessment for Writing** (Handouts 18A and 18B) as well as the **Standards for Reasoning** (Handout 18D) to guide discussion. Students may also meet with the teacher for discussion and comments, guided by the **Teacher Assessment for Writing** (Handout 18C). Provide time for students to revise their papers.

5. Remind students that they will be making an oral presentation about their issue later in the unit (Lesson 22).

NOTE TO TEACHER

The process of drafting and revising the paper on the research issue should not be undertaken in one class session. The activities described in this lesson may be carried out over the course of several days, interspersed with the surrounding lessons.

HOMEWORK

Do a final editing of your paper and make a final draft either by hand or on a word processor.

JOURNEYS AND DESTINATIONS

Self-Assessment for Writing
(Handout 18A)

NAME: _____ DATE: _____

ASSIGNMENT: _____

Directions: Grade your own writing. For each sentence below, circle the choice that describes your writing best.

1. My main idea is clear.	Needs Improvement	Satisfactory	Excellent
2. My details support the main idea.	Needs Improvement	Satisfactory	Excellent
3. My ideas flow smoothly and orderly.	Needs Improvement	Satisfactory	Excellent
4. The hamburger paragraph structure is clear (introduction, body, conclusion).	Needs Improvement	Satisfactory	Excellent
5. My vocabulary is rich and varied.	Needs Improvement	Satisfactory	Excellent

MY WRITING IS STRONG IN THESE WAYS:

_____

_____

_____

MY WRITING COULD BE IMPROVED IN THESE WAYS:

_____

_____

_____

Peer Assessment for Writing
(Handout 18B)

READER: _____ WRITER: _____

ASSIGNMENT: _____

Directions: Read your partner's writing sample carefully. For each sentence below, circle the choice that you think describes the writing.

1. The main idea is clear.	Needs Improvement	Satisfactory	Excellent
2. The details support the main idea.	Needs Improvement	Satisfactory	Excellent
3. The ideas flow smoothly and orderly.	Needs Improvement	Satisfactory	Excellent
4. The hamburger paragraph structure is clear (introduction, body, conclusion).	Needs Improvement	Satisfactory	Excellent
5. The vocabulary is rich and varied.	Needs Improvement	Satisfactory	Excellent

THE WRITING SAMPLE IS STRONG IN THESE WAYS:

_____

_____

_____

THE WRITING SAMPLE COULD BE IMPROVED IN THESE WAYS:

_____

_____

_____

Teacher Assessment for Writing
(Handout 18C)

STUDENT: _____ DATE: _____

ASSIGNMENT: _____

Directions: Circle the words that best describe the writing.

1. The main idea is clear.	Needs Improvement	Satisfactory	Excellent
2. Appropriate level of detail is provided to support the main idea.	Needs Improvement	Satisfactory	Excellent
3. The ideas flow smoothly and orderly.	Needs Improvement	Satisfactory	Excellent
4. The hamburger paragraph structure is clear (introduction, body, conclusion).	Needs Improvement	Satisfactory	Excellent
5. The writing uses descriptive language and rich vocabulary.	Needs Improvement	Satisfactory	Excellent
Optional: Demonstrates correct grammar, usage, and mechanics.	Needs Improvement	Satisfactory	Excellent

PARTICULAR STRENGTHS:

_____

_____

AREAS NEEDING IMPROVEMENT:

_____

_____

Standards for Reasoning

(Handout 18D)

NAME: _____ DATE: _____

Use these questions to think about the reasoning used in a hamburger paragraph:

▼ Are there **enough reasons** to make a convincing argument? One or two reasons might not be enough to show someone your point of view well enough for them to understand it.

▼ Is the evidence **correct or right**? Teachers might not agree that "Most of the homework is busy work."

▼ Are the reasons **clear**? Is the meaning understandable by anyone who reads this?

▼ Are **specific** reasons or examples included rather than vague generalizations? "It would help me learn to be responsible" alone is too general. "I would have to feed it and take it for a walk every day" is more specific and helps strengthen the argument in the dog paragraph. How specific are the reasons in the homework paragraph?

▼ Are the arguments and reasons **strong and important**, or do they seem to be included just to have something to say?

▼ Is the thinking **logical**? Does the paragraph follow an understandable path or is it just a disconnected group of statements? Do the sentences seem to go together and to be in the right order?

LESSON
19
▼

Sachiko Means Happiness

CURRICULUM ALIGNMENT CODE

GOAL 1	GOAL 2	GOAL 3	GOAL 4	GOAL 5	GOAL 6
X	X	X		X	X

INSTRUCTIONAL PURPOSE

▼ To develop reasoning and interpretive skills in literature through discussing the story *Sachiko Means Happiness*.

▼ To explore new vocabulary words.

▼ To explore interdisciplinary connections with art and social studies through discussion of Chinese and Japanese culture.

MATERIALS USED

1. *Sachiko Means Happiness* by Kimiko Sakai*

2. Student **Response Journals**

3. Literature Web—Primary Adaptation (Handout 19A)

4. Vocabulary Web (Handout 19B)

5. Change Matrix (Handout 3B, from Lesson 3)

6. *Emma's Dragon Hunt* by Catherine Stock** (to be read aloud)

7. Globes and/or world maps

8. Selected books and magazines containing reprints of Chinese and Japanese art

9. Selected resources about the cultures of China and Japan

*Sakai, K. (1990). *Sachiko means happiness*. San Francisco, CA: Children's Book Press.

**Stock, C. (1984). *Emma's dragon hunt*. New York: Lothrop, Lee, and Shepard.

ACTIVITIES

1. Recall the lesson in which students compared themselves at different ages. Engage the students in a discussion of **How People Change** as they age. Use pictures of famous people at different ages to illustrate this point.

2. Explain that the story for this session is called *Sachiko Means Happiness* and focuses on how Sachiko's grandmother has changed. Read the story to the students.

3. Have students work in groups to do a **Literature Web** (Handout 19A) for *Sachiko Means Happiness.*

4. Discuss the story, using the following questions.

Literary Response and Interpretation Questions

▼ *At the beginning of the story Sachiko says, "I don't like sunsets; trouble always begins in the evening." Explain possible meanings of this sentence. What happens in the evening that Sachiko does not like?*

▼ *Sachiko and Grandmother have the same name. How does the meaning of their name relate to how they feel in the story?*

▼ *Why does Sachiko invite Grandmother to stay with her tonight when she already lives at Sachiko's house?*

▼ *When Sachiko and Grandmother look at the sunset at the end of the story, Sachiko thinks it is beautiful, and now she likes it. Why did her opinion of the sunset change? What might the sunset be a symbol for?*

Reasoning Questions

▼ *Why do you think the author wrote this story? What about the story suggests the author's purpose to you?*

Change Questions

▼ *Describe how Grandmother and Sachiko have changed.*

▼ *How are the five generalizations about change brought out in this story?*

5. Have students work in groups to complete a **Vocabulary Web** (Handout 19B) for one of the following words from *Sachiko Means Happiness*: **impatiently, crossly, reassure, timidly, reflected.**

6. In your **Response Journal** respond to one of the following questions:

   ▼ *If you were Sachiko, what would you do to make Grandmother feel better?*

   ▼ *Do you have any elderly friends or relatives who seem not to remember you sometimes? How does that feel? What can you do to help in that situation?*

7. As a whole class activity, complete the column of the **Change Matrix** (Handout 3B) that applies to this reading. Have students complete their copy of the Matrix as well as filling in the butcher paper or posterboard copy. The completed grid will serve as the basis for a discussion in a later lesson about change.

8. Read *Emma's Dragon Hunt* by Catherine Stock aloud. As a class, make a Venn diagram comparing Sachiko's relationship with her grandmother to Emma's relationship with her grandfather. Discuss, using the following questions as a guide:

   ▼ *How do the girls each feel about their grandparent at the beginning of the story? Why do they feel the way they do?*

   ▼ *What happens in each story to change the way the main characters feel?*

   ▼ *Sachiko's grandmother and Emma's grandfather are both changing. How do the generalizations about change apply to their lives? In what ways are their changes similar? In what ways are their changes different?*

9. Explain to students that *Sachiko Means Happiness* is about a Japanese American family and *Emma's Dragon Hunt* is about a Chinese American family. Have students locate both Japan and China on a map or globe. Direct students' attention to the art panels along the sides of pages in *Sachiko Means Happiness* and to the artwork on the kites in *Emma's Dragon Hunt*. Divide students into groups and provide each group with selections of traditional artwork from both nations in books, magazines, or other sources. Have each group study the artwork and list ways in which the artwork of the two nations are similar and ways in which they are different. Discuss ideas as a class.

10. Use the discussion of Chinese and Japanese art as a springboard for further investigation of the two cultures. Working individually or in small groups, students may select a topic such as food, language, architecture, school, or family to investigate about one or both cultures. Work with a media specialist to gather resources which will help students in this endeavor. Have students report their findings to

the class, and discuss how and why the two cultures are similar to and different from each other. Also, consider in discussion how each of the cultures has influenced American culture.

EXTENSIONS

1. Choose a wordless picture book to use as a basis for creating your own story. Organize your understanding of the story by writing notes about the purpose, the sequence of events, and the ending on note cards. Also make note cards to identify characters and setting. Write a one to two-page story, using your note cards to guide your thinking.

2. If you enjoyed reading *Sachiko Means Happiness* and *Emma's Dragon Hunt*, you may enjoy reading these books about Asian Americans:

   Bunting, E. (1982). *The happy funeral*. New York: HarperCollins.

   Coutant, H. (1974). *First snow*. New York: Knopf.

   Friedman, I. R. (1984). *How my parents learned to eat*. New York: Houghton Mifflin.

   Levine, E. (1989). *I hate English!* New York: Scholastic.

   Lord, B. B. (1984). *In the year of the boar and Jackie Robinson*. New York: HarperCollins.

3. Try to find out what your name means. Explain in your **Response Journal** how you think your name's meaning fits or does not fit you.

Literature Web—
Primary Adaptation
(Handout 19A)

NAME: _____ DATE: _____

Key Words

Feelings

Reading

Ideas

Images or Symbols

JOURNEYS
AND
DESTINATIONS

Vocabulary Web
(Handout 19B)

NAME: _____ DATE: _____

Synonyms:

Sentence:

Definition:

Antonyms:

Word:

Part of Speech:

Example:

Analysis

Word Families:

Stems:

Origin:

LESSON
20
Oral Presentation Practice

CURRICULUM ALIGNMENT CODE

GOAL 1	GOAL 2	GOAL 3	GOAL 4	GOAL 5	GOAL 6
			X		

INSTRUCTIONAL PURPOSE

▼ To develop listening/oral communication skills, including oral presentation strategies.

MATERIALS USED

1. Oral Presentation Evaluation Form (Handout 20A)

2. Note cards

3. Change Matrix (Handout 3B, from Lesson 3)

ACTIVITIES

1. Remind students that they will give a **Presentation** during Lesson 22 on their issue of what is the best way to preserve memories (see Lessons 10 and 17). Explain that they will base their presentation on the papers they have written about the issue.

2. Generate with students a list of ideas on the topic of "things to remember about giving an oral presentation." Establish two categories for ideas, one dealing with *organization* or *preparation of material*, the other with *delivery*. If necessary, supplement student suggestions with key ideas such as:

   a) Speak loudly and clearly so you can be understood.

   b) Make eye contact with your audience.

   c) State the purpose of your presentation.

d) Illustrate your ideas with examples.

e) End with a strong, interesting idea that restates the purpose of your presentation.

3. Distribute copies of the **Oral Presentation Evaluation Form** (Handout 20A) and discuss the criteria which should be used in judging oral presentations. Ask students to think about these criteria as they prepare their presentations.

4. Ask students to select a character they find interesting from one of the unit's stories. Allow about ten minutes for students to prepare a **1–2 Minute Talk** about the character. Have students include a **Description of the Character**; tell why they find him/her interesting; tell how the character changes or does not change during the story. Encourage students to look back at the stories and use their **Change Matrix** (Handout 3B) to prepare their presentations. Students' notes may be organized on a set of index cards, one containing key phrases which describe the character, another explaining the student's feelings about the character, a third explaining how the character changed in the story, and a fourth how the character did not change.

5. Organize students into small groups to give their presentations. Each group should listen to all presentations from group members, then discuss what was most effective about the presentations and how the presentations might be improved. Students should refer to the class-generated list of "Things to Remember" and the **Oral Presentation Evaluation Form** to guide their discussion.

HOMEWORK

1. Prepare an oral presentation on the issue of how to preserve memories. Use your written work to guide your oral presentation. Prepare a note card labeled **Point of View**, which explains your opinion on the issue, cards for each of your **Reasons**, and a card for your **Conclusion**.

2. Practice your oral presentation at home, remembering the tips discussed in class.

Oral Presentation Evaluation Form

(Handout 20A)

SPEAKER: _____ DATE: _____

ASSIGNMENT: _____

Directions: Circle the choice that describes each of the following best.

ORGANIZATION

1. The purpose of the presentation was clear.	Needs Improvement	Satisfactory	Excellent
2. The speaker included good examples.	Needs Improvement	Satisfactory	Excellent
3. The speaker showed knowledge of the subject.	Needs Improvement	Satisfactory	Excellent
4. The presentation closed with a strong, interesting idea that restated the purpose.	Needs Improvement	Satisfactory	Excellent

DELIVERY

1. The speaker made good eye contact with the audience.	Needs Improvement	Satisfactory	Excellent
2. The presentation was loud enough.	Needs Improvement	Satisfactory	Excellent
3. The speaker's words were clear enough to be understood.	Needs Improvement	Satisfactory	Excellent

THE BEST PART OF THIS PRESENTATION WAS:

_____

_____

A SUGGESTION FOR IMPROVEMENT IS:

_____

_____

LESSON
21
The Green Man

CURRICULUM ALIGNMENT CODE

GOAL 1	GOAL 2	GOAL 3	GOAL 4	GOAL 5	GOAL 6
X		X		X	X

INSTRUCTIONAL PURPOSE

▼ To develop reasoning and interpretation skills through discussing *The Green Man*.

▼ To explore new vocabulary words.

▼ To explore the concept of change in literature.

MATERIALS USED

1. *The Green Man* by Gail E. Haley*

2. Student **Response Journals**

3. Literature Web—Primary Adaptation (Handout 21A)

4. Vocabulary Web (Handout 21B)

5. Change Matrix (Handout 3B)

ACTIVITIES

1. Distribute copies of *The Green Man*. Have students read the story.

2. Have students work individually to complete a **Literature Web** (Handout 21A) for *The Green Man*. Discuss as a class.

3. Continue discussion using these questions.

*Haley, G. E. (1988). *The green man*. Blowing Rock, NC: New River.

Literary Response and Interpretation Questions

▼ *Who is the green man in the story? Why is he important to people?*

▼ *What does Claude learn in the forest? What does he learn about surviving? What does he learn about himself? What does he learn about life?*

▼ *What are some main ideas in this story? What idea do you think is the most important one?*

▼ *In the first paragraph on page 26, what do you think the following sentence means? "Even the sun and the moon seemed to smile upon him."*

Reasoning Questions

▼ *What does protection mean? Who protects whom in the story? How does the concept of protection relate to the story?*

▼ *What evidence is there in the story that Claude became the green man?*

▼ *What reasons would you give for Claude changing his ways in the story?*

▼ *Create a different title for this story. List two reasons based on the reading.*

Change Questions

▼ *Did Claude change from the inside out or the outside in? Defend your point of view.*

▼ *What does the author tell you about change in this story? Support what you say with details from the story.*

4. In your **Response Journal** respond to one of the following questions:

▼ *Why do we believe in things that we cannot see? Give an example and write about it.*

▼ *Is it easier to change things about yourself on the outside or the inside? Why?*

5. Have students work in groups to complete a **Vocabulary Web** (Handout 21B) for one of the following words from *The Green Man*: **glean, defiant, tether, arrogant.**

6. As a whole class activity, complete the column of the **Change Matrix** (Handout 3B) that applies to this reading. Have students complete their copy of the Matrix as well as filling in the butcher paper or posterboard copy. The completed grid will serve as the basis for a discussion in a later lesson about change.

7. Close the session by reviewing expectations for oral presentations, based on the **Oral Presentation Evaluation Form** and class discussions (refer to Lesson 20), and encouraging students to practice their presentations on their memory research with a parent.

HOMEWORK

1. Practice for the oral presentation on what is the best way to preserve memories.

2. Review unit vocabulary words.

3. Write a story about change in your life or in the life of someone close to you. Think about our generalizations about change and the different stories we have studied about change as you plan your story. The story will be used for an activity in Lesson 23.

EXTENSION

1. If you enjoyed reading *The Green Man*, you may enjoy reading other books by G. E. Haley

   Haley, G. E. (1984). *Birdsong*. New York: Crown.

   Haley, G. E. (1977). *Go away, stay away*. New York: Scribner's.

   Haley, G. E. (1986). *Jack and the bean tree*. New York: Crown.

   Haley, G. E. (1988). *Jack and the fire dragon*. New York: Crown.

2. Read *The Adventures of Robin Hood* by Howard Pyle. How was this character like the Green Man? Make a visual to compare the two, and prepare an oral presentation of your ideas.

Literature Web—
Primary Adaptation

(Handout 21A)

NAME: _____ DATE: _____

Key Words

Feelings

Reading

Ideas

Images or
Symbols

Vocabulary Web
(Handout 21B)

NAME: _____ DATE: _____

Synonyms:

Sentence:

Definition:

Antonyms:

Word:

Part of Speech:

Example:

Analysis

Word Families:

Stems:

Origin:

LESSON

22

Presentation of Research

CURRICULUM ALIGNMENT CODE

GOAL 1	GOAL 2	GOAL 3	GOAL 4	GOAL 5	GOAL 6
		X	X		X

INSTRUCTIONAL PURPOSE

▼ To present projects related to students' research on how to preserve memories.

▼ To review unit vocabulary.

MATERIALS USED

1. Video Recorder

2. Student-prepared note cards

3. Oral Presentation Evaluation Form (Handout 22A)

ACTIVITIES

1. Allow students to give their oral presentations on the research issue. Videotape the presentations. Use the **Oral Presentation Evaluation Form** (Handout 22A) to assess student presentations.

2. Encourage class discussion of the project based on the following questions.

    ▼ *Where did you locate most of your resources?*

    ▼ *What would you do differently next time (research, product, presentation)?*

    ▼ *What was the hardest part of this assignment?*

    ▼ *What have you learned?*

207

3. Do a **Lightning Round** on the vocabulary studied throughout the unit as a final vocabulary review. (See Lesson 7 for description of the Lightning Round activity.)

NOTE TO TEACHER

The Lightning Round Activity may be used as a culminating vocabulary activity, as well as an ongoing assessment of linguistic competency in vocabulary throughout the unit.

HOMEWORK

Revise and edit your story about a person's change in your life. Prepare a clean copy of your story for the next lesson.

Oral Presentation Evaluation Form
(Handout 22A)

SPEAKER: _____ DATE: _____

ASSIGNMENT: _____

Directions: Circle the choice that describes each of the following best.

ORGANIZATION

1. The purpose of the presentation was clear.	Needs Improvement	Satisfactory	Excellent
2. The speaker included good examples.	Needs Improvement	Satisfactory	Excellent
3. The speaker showed knowledge of the subject.	Needs Improvement	Satisfactory	Excellent
4. The presentation closed with a strong, interesting idea that restated the purpose.	Needs Improvement	Satisfactory	Excellent

DELIVERY

1. The speaker made good eye contact with the audience.	Needs Improvement	Satisfactory	Excellent
2. The presentation was loud enough.	Needs Improvement	Satisfactory	Excellent
3. The speaker's words were clear enough to be understood.	Needs Improvement	Satisfactory	Excellent

THE BEST PART OF THIS PRESENTATION WAS:

_____

_____

A SUGGESTION FOR IMPROVEMENT IS:

_____

_____

LESSON

23

Closing Discussion of the Concept of Change

CURRICULUM ALIGNMENT CODE

GOAL 1	GOAL 2	GOAL 3	GOAL 4	GOAL 5	GOAL 6
	X				X

INSTRUCTIONAL PURPOSE

▼ To assess student understanding of the generalizations about change.

▼ To discuss the unit guiding question, "How does change help us grow?"

▼ To develop persuasive writing skills.

MATERIALS USED

1. Change Matrix (Handout 3B, from Lesson 3)

2. Student **Response Journals**

3. Final Writing Assignment (Handout 23A)

ACTIVITIES

1. Students were asked to come to class with a story about change in their own lives or a change in the life of someone else. Have students share their stories in small groups. (The stories were assigned as homework in Lesson 21 and revised for homework in Lesson 22.)

2. While they are in their small groups, have students complete the **Change Matrix** (Handout 3B) on the literature used in the unit and their own story.

3. Use the Change Matrix as the basis for a whole class discussion synthesizing unit learning. Guide the discussion with questions such as those listed below:

- ▼ *How were the changes in Michael in "Shells" similar to the changes in Sachiko? What did each of them learn? How did the changes in them come about?*

- ▼ *Compare the changes in Claude in* The Green Man *to the changes in the main character of "The Ugly Duckling." In which character were there more outside changes? In which character were there more inside changes?*

- ▼ *What did the main characters of* The Green Book *and* The Green Man *do that changed the way others thought of them? How did their relationships change?*

- ▼ *Describe how changes in nature brought about changes in the characters' lives in* Bringing the Rain to Kapiti Plain *and in* The Green Book.

- ▼ *Think about how you have changed from reading the stories and poems in this unit. Which selection changed you the most? How did it change you?*

- ▼ *Which character(s) in the stories we read changed in a similar way to the person in the story you wrote? How were they alike, and how were they different?*

- ▼ *What special skills did the characters have to learn to survive their problem situations in the different stories? In what ways were these survival skills alike and different?*

4. Revisit the five generalizations on change, discussing examples of how the ideas about change were illustrated in the literature of the unit.

- ▼ *Change is linked to time. (How is change linked to time?)*

- ▼ *Change may be positive or negative. (Does change always represent progress?)*

- ▼ *Change may be perceived as orderly or random. (Can we predict change?)*

- ▼ *Change is everywhere. (Does change apply to all areas of our world?)*

- ▼ *Change may happen naturally or may be caused by people. (What causes change?)*

5. Divide students into five small groups. Assign each group one of the change generalizations. Allow 10–15 minutes of discussion within the groups to address the following question as it relates to that generalization. Students should take notes on the discussion.

 ▼ *How have the experiences of this unit supported the generalization?*

6. Have students share their findings in a whole class discussion.

7. Distribute copies of the **Final Writing Assignment** (Handout 23A) and discuss the assignment. Students are to select one of the generalizations about change and write a persuasive paragraph to argue that it is true, based on the literature studied in the unit. Students may use their individual Change Matrix and the class Change Matrix as well as other notes from the unit to assist them in developing their paragraphs.

8. Have students re-read all products in their portfolios and **Response Journals** and write a response to the following question

 ▼ *How have your written products changed during this unit?*

NOTE TO TEACHER

The writing assignment given in this lesson serves a dual purpose. It may be used as an additional assessment of student persuasive writing skills, as well as providing a closing unit assessment on the concept of change.

Final Writing Assignment
(Handout 23A)

NAME: _____ DATE: _____

Think about how the literature pieces you have read in this unit have reflected the five generalizations about change. Select one generalization which seemed especially true to you in the unit readings and write it below. List examples from several of the readings of how the generalization was true in those pieces of literature. Use at least three **different** stories or poems from the unit.

Generalization:

Examples:

      Write a persuasive paragraph arguing that the generalization you selected is true, based on the examples from the literature. State your opinion on the issue, then give at least three reasons which show evidence that the generalization is true. Explain your reasons thoroughly. Write a conclusion to end your paragraph.

LESSON
24

Post-Assessment of Literature Interpretation and Persuasive Writing

CURRICULUM ALIGNMENT CODE					
GOAL 1	GOAL 2	GOAL 3	GOAL 4	GOAL 5	GOAL 6
X	X			X	X

INSTRUCTIONAL PURPOSE

▼ To develop reasoning and interpretation skills in literature by discussing the story "The Miser."

▼ To administer the unit post-assessments in literature and writing.

▼ To assess student progress on unit goals.

MATERIALS USED

1. "The Miser"

2. Literature Post-Assessment (Handout 24A)

3. Literature Interpretation Scoring Rubric for Pre- and Post-Assessments

4. Persuasive Writing Post-Assessment (Handout 24B)

5. Persuasive Writing Scoring Rubric for Pre- and Post-Assessments

6. Overall Student Assessment Report (Handout 24C)

ACTIVITIES

1. Have students read the story "The Miser" and take the **Post-Assessment for Literature** (Handout 24A).

2. Have students keep their papers and the story and discuss the post-assessment questions.

3. Collect the **Post-Assessments for Literature**.

4. Distribute the **Post-Assessment for Writing**. Have students complete the post-assessment. Discuss the post-assessment for writing question. After the discussion, collect the papers.

NOTES TO TEACHER

1. *Compare individual assessment papers to each student's pre-assessment papers for literature and for writing to give you a basis for citing improvement that has taken place. Comparing scores may not adequately or definitively reflect the changes that have occurred. The rubrics included with the lesson may be used to provide the basis for scoring student responses.*

2. *Use the **Overall Student Assessment Report** (Handout 24C) to rate student progress on each goal from participation in the unit.*

Literature Post-Assessment
(Handout 24A)

NAME: _____ DATE: _____

Please read the passage and answer the questions.

1. State an important idea of the story in a sentence or two.

2. In your own words describe what you think the author means by the words, "A possession is worth no more than the use we make of it."

3. What does the story tell us about the idea of change? Support what you say with details from the story.

4. Create a title for this story. Give two reasons from the story for your new title.

Literature Interpretation Scoring Rubric for Pre- and Post-Assessments

1. **State an important idea of the reading in a sentence or two.**

Score	Description of Response
1	limited, vague, inaccurate, confusing, only quotes from reading
2	simplistic, literal statement; uses only part of main idea; creates title rather than main idea
3	insightful, addresses theme

2. **Use your own words to describe what you think the author means by . . .**

Score	Description of Response
1	limited, vague, inaccurate; rewording only
2	accurate but literal response
3	insightful, interpretive response

3. **What does the story tell us about the idea of change? Support what you say with details from the story.**

Score	Description of Response
1	limited, vague, inaccurate; only quotes from story
2	valid generalization without support **or** well-supported example
3	valid generalization about change is made and well supported

4. **Create a title for this story. Give two reasons from the story for your new title.**

Score	Description of Response
1	limited, vague, or title given without reasons
2	appropriate but literal response; at least one reason given
3	insightful, meaningful title given with support

Sample Student Responses
Post-Assessment for Literature

1. **State an important idea of the reading in a sentence or two.**

    SAMPLE 1-POINT RESPONSES:

    - *A possession is no more than what you make of it.*

    - *He is greedy and mean.*

    SAMPLE 2-POINT RESPONSE:

    - *You should always use the things you have.*

    SAMPLE 3-POINT RESPONSE:

    - *If you don't ever use something it's just no good, so spend it if you need to.*

2. **Use your own words to describe what you think the author means by . . .**

    SAMPLE 1-POINT RESPONSE:

    - *Possessions are not good, they are the same as a stone.*

    SAMPLE 2-POINT RESPONSE:

    - *I think it means the gold that the miser owned is worth nothing because he didn't use it for anything.*

    SAMPLE 3-POINT RESPONSE:

    - *It doesn't matter how much you have, what matters is if you use it the right way.*

3. **What does the story tell us about the idea of change? Support with details.**

    SAMPLE 1-POINT RESPONSE:

    - *The gold was underground and then it was robbed by a robber.*

    SAMPLE 2-POINT RESPONSE:

    - *I think this story's change is that the Miser first had his gold and then lost it, so it changed from positive to negative.*

    SAMPLE 3-POINT RESPONSE:

    - *The author shows that change can be caused by people because the robber made a change by taking the Miser's gold.*

4. **Create a title for this story. Give two reasons from the story for your new title.**

SAMPLE 1-POINT RESPONSE:

- *The Miser's Gold. I say this because there was a miser and he had gold.*

SAMPLE 2-POINT RESPONSE:

- *A good title for this story is "Possessions" because the miser doesn't use his possession and learns his lesson and this story is about the miser's possession.*

SAMPLE 3-POINT RESPONSE:

- *The Thief's Treasure. I would pick this title because the thief would probably have made more use of the money than the miser.*

Persuasive Writing Post-Assessment
(Handout 24B)

NAME: _____ DATE: _____

Directions: Write a paragraph to answer the question below. State your opinion, include three reasons for your opinion, and write a conclusion to your paragraph.

Do you think the story, "The Miser," should be required reading for all students in your grade?

Persuasive Writing Scoring Rubric for Pre- and Post-Assessments

Claim or Opinion

Score	Description of Response
0	No clear position exists on the writer's assertion, preference, or view, and context does not help clarify it.
2	Yes/no alone or writer's position is poorly formulated, but reader is reasonably sure what the paper is about because of context.
4	A basic topic sentence exists, and the reader is reasonably sure what the paper is about based on the strength of the topic sentence alone.
6	A very clear, concise position is given as a topic sentence, and the reader is very certain what the paper is about. Must include details such as grade level, title of the reading, or reference to "the story," etc.

Data or Supporting Points

Score	Description of Response
0	No data are offered that are relevant to the claim.
2	Scant data (one or two pieces) are offered, but what data exist are relevant to the claim.
4	At least three pieces of data are offered. They are relevant but not necessarily convincing or complete.
6	At least three pieces of accurate and convincing data are offered.

Warrant or Elaboration on Data

Score	Description of Response
0	No warrant or elaboration is offered.
2	An attempt is made to elaborate at least one element of the data.
4	More than one piece of data is explained, but the explanation is weak and lacks thoroughness, **or** one piece of data is well elaborated.
6	The writer explains more than one piece of data in such a way that it is clear how they support the argument. At least one piece of data is convincingly and completely elaborated.

(Adapted from N. Burkhalter, 1995)

Conclusion

Score	Description of Response
0	No conclusion/closing sentence is provided.
2	A conclusion/closing sentence is provided.

Sample Student Responses
Post-Assessment for Writing

Sample 1

I think everyone in my grade should be required to read the Miser because well, for these reasons. One is because it is a great story, it tells a good lesson for third graders to learn. It shows how you use your treasures wisely, or they are not really worth anything. Another reason is third graders would also like the story and want to read it. You don't have to agree with my opinion, but I believe everyone in my grade should read this short story.

Score: **Claim = 4**   **Total Score = 10**
        Data = 2
        Warrant = 2
        Conclusion = 2

Sample 2

I do think that the story "The Miser" should be required reading for all students in my grade because it teaches a good lesson. It tells you that if you don't use your things they're as useless as a rock and you should keep your things in a safe place. This is why I think that the story "The Miser" should be required reading for all students in my grade.

Score: **Claim = 6**   **Total Score = 14**
        Data = 2
        Warrant = 4
        Conclusion = 2

Sample 3

Yes, I think all the students in 3rd grade should read this book. It's such an excellent moral. One reason I think everyone in third grade should read "The Miser" is because it does teach a good lesson. It could help them learn that things they never use are worthless. Another reason I think all the students in third grade should read this story is they use great, funny words. It basically is a funny story. One of the parts I liked was "He pulled his hair out" (not really). It would make our writing better. Also, the students should read this because it's similar to a true story. If you have a good, healthy body and you never use it, the muscles will be very weak, and you'll miss out on a lot of things. As you see, it's a good moral for all the students in third grade. They could learn great details for their own stories, and they can compare it with a true happening like this story. It's a great story!

Score: **Claim = 6**   **Total Score = 20**
        Data = 6
        Warrant = 6
        Conclusion = 2

Overall Student Assessment Report

(Handout 24C)

NAME: _____ DATE: _____

Directions: Please rate each of the following using the scale: 3 = Excellent; 2 = Satisfactory; 1 = Needs Improvement. Also, write a brief narrative assessing the student's ability, progress, or other pertinent information.

	Needs Improvement	Satisfactory	Excellent
GOAL #1—INTERPRETATION OF LITERATURE			
—Pre-assessment for literature	1	2	3
—Literature webs	1	2	3
—Quality of literature discussion	1	2	3
—Post-assessment for literature	1	2	3
GOAL #2—WRITING			
—Pre-assessment for writing	1	2	3
—Persuasive writing	1	2	3
—Literary response writings	1	2	3
—Writing assignment on ways to remember	1	2	3
—Diamante poem	1	2	3
—Post-assessment for writing	1	2	3
GOAL #3—GRAMMAR/VOCABULARY			
—Vocabulary webs	1	2	3
—Correct use of parts of speech in diamante poem	1	2	3

	Needs Improvement	Satisfactory	Excellent
GOAL #4—LISTENING/SPEAKING			
—Small/large group discussion	1	2	3
—Presentation on wordless picture book (Lesson 14)	1	2	3
—Presentation about story character (Lesson 20)	1	2	3
—Student presentation based on ways of remembering project	1	2	3
GOAL #5—REASONING			
—Venn diagrams	1	2	3
—Discussion/application of elements and standards of reasoning	1	2	3
GOAL #6—CHANGE			
—Change matrix	1	2	3
—Writing about change (Handout 11A)	1	2	3
—Final writing assignment on change (Handout 23A)	1	2	3
MAJOR PROJECTS			
—Research project on ways to remember	1	2	3

Briefly comment on the student's progress in understanding the concept of "change."

_____

_____

_____

Briefly comment on the student's progress in reasoning ability.

_____

_____

_____

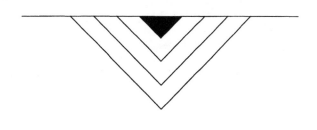

SECTION

III

IMPLEMENTATION

This section includes guidelines for unit implementation in classrooms and outlines the instructional models employed in the unit.

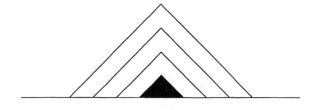

▼ Classroom Guidelines

The following pages outline some guidelines for teachers in implementing the unit effectively in classrooms. Feedback from teachers who piloted the unit has been used in developing these recommendations.

Target Population

This unit was designed for use with high ability second and third grade students. It has been piloted with such students in various settings and found effective with respect to learning gains. In heterogeneous settings, the unit has been used with a broader range of students and found effective as well, provided that teachers have modified the reading selections.

Use of the Unit in Relation to Existing Language Arts Curriculum

This unit is intended to replace a semester's work in language arts for high ability learners. Thus, whoever teaches the unit should assign grades for language arts and note individual progress based on the goals of the unit. (See Overall Student Assessment Report at the end of the unit lesson plans.) Because the unit does not include specific lesson emphasis on spelling, developmental reading skills, or narrative writing, it is recommended that these elements be considered for use during a second semester of language arts. Supplemental materials to be used might include *Junior Great Books, Write Source 2000, The Magic Lens*, and *Word within a Word*. (See Section IV, Bibliography, for citations.)

Alignment of the Unit with National Standards

This unit of study has been aligned with the English standards developed by the National Council of Teachers of English (NCTE) and the International Reading Association (IRA). It responds to all major aspects of those standards, while incorporating a rigorous assessment component to enhance individual student progress during and at the conclusion of the unit. The alignment process has also been done for individual state documents in language arts, including Connecticut, New York, South Carolina, Texas, and Virginia. Selected district alignments have also been completed.

The chart on the following page represents the NCTE/IRA alignment:

Alignment with NCTE/IRA Standards

Standards for the English Language Arts	William & Mary Language Arts Units
1. Students read a wide range of print and nonprint texts to build an understanding of texts, of themselves, and of the cultures of the United States and the world; to acquire new information; to respond to the needs and demands of society and the workplace; and for personal fulfillment.	Emphasis on multicultural and global literature and broad-based reading.
2. Students read a wide range of literature from many periods in many genres to build an understanding of the many dimensions (e.g., philosophical, ethical, aesthetic) of human experience.	Broad-based reading in poetry, short story, biography, essay, and novel forms.
3. Students apply a wide range of strategies to comprehend, interpret, evaluate, and appreciate texts.	Major goal on analysis and interpretation of literature. (Goal #1)
4. Students adjust their use of spoken, written, and visual language to communicate effectively with a variety of audiences and for different purposes.	Sensitivity to audience built into writing and research activities.
5. Students employ a wide range of strategies as they write and use different writing process elements appropriately.	Major outcome related to effective use of all stages of the writing process. (Goal #2)
6. Students apply knowledge of language structure, language conventions, media techniques, figurative language, and genre to create, critique, and discuss print and nonprint texts.	Major goal of developing linguistic competency. (Goal #3)
7. Students conduct research on issues and interests by generating ideas and questions, and by posing problems. They gather, evaluate, and synthesize data from a variety of sources to communicate their discoveries in ways that suit their purpose and audience.	Research project that focuses on these skills based on issue identification is a feature of each unit; the use of the reasoning model underlies the teaching of all language arts strands. (Goal #5)
8. Students use a wide variety of technological and informational resources to gather and synthesize information and to create and communicate knowledge.	Incorporated in research model and writing task demands.
9. Students develop an understanding of and respect for diversity in language use, patterns, and dialects across cultures, ethnic groups, geographic regions, and social roles.	Applicable to the context of selected literature.
10. Students whose first language is not English make use of their first language to develop competency in the English language arts and understanding of content across the curriculum.	N/A
11. Students participate as knowledgeable, reflective, creative, and critical members of a variety of literacy communities.	Contact with authors, use of peer review, major discussions of literary works.
12. Students use spoken, written, and visual language to accomplish their own purposes.	Integrated throughout the units.

Schedule for Unit Implementation

For the purposes of this unit, a lesson is defined as at least one two-hour session. It is preferable that the unit be taught across a two-hour block that encompasses both reading and language arts time allocations. A minimum of forty total instructional hours should be allocated for teaching this unit. Teachers are encouraged to expand this schedule based on available time and student interest. Many teachers have used the unit for a full semester of work. Ideally, this curriculum should be taught in a setting in which the class meets on a daily basis.

Grouping

The unit has been implemented in a variety of classroom grouping models, including heterogeneous classrooms, pull-out programs, and self-contained gifted classes. Based on our feedback from national pilots, we suggest that school districts employ their existing grouping approach to teach the unit the first time. Based on individual district results from the first year of implementation, decisions about regrouping procedures may be explored. The comments that follow relate to implementation tips for each setting:

Inclusion or Heterogeneous Classrooms

▼ In this type of setting, it is recommended that teachers differentiate the readings for implementation. Unit readings are clearly intended for advanced readers.

▼ It is also advisable to cluster group students based on reading selections for discussion of these readings.

▼ All students can benefit from learning the fundamental teaching models employed in the unit.

▼ The research project may be modified for students, based on individual levels of functioning.

Pull-out Programs

▼ Students must meet at least two hours per week in order for this unit to be implemented successfully.

▼ Consider cross-grade grouping in order to implement this unit.

▼ Continuity of ideas is the challenge in implementing this unit. It is essential that homework be assigned and completed, even within a pull-out program that does not meet daily.

▼ In this setting, the unit needs to be supplemented with other materials and resources. Use of *Junior Great Books* to enhance literature study is recommended. Michael Thompson's materials in vocabulary and grammar are also recommended (see bibliography for suggestions).

▼ Cluster grouping is encouraged to ensure that advanced readers are grouped together.

Use of Learning Centers

Learning Centers should be set up and made available for student use throughout the course of the unit. They help to provide a change of pace during large time blocks of instruction as well as allowing students to explore topics of interest more fully. They are introduced in the lesson plans as they become relevant to the aspects of the unit being studied. (See below for indication of the lessons in which each Center is introduced.) Learning Centers may be managed as the teacher sees fit, with specific times assigned to Center activities or on a less structured basis. It would be helpful to have an assistant to interact with students and answer questions during Center time. Some recording system should be established for each Center, whether students will keep records in their own unit notebooks or in a notebook to be left at the Center.

a. **Unit Vocabulary Center** (Lesson 4)

At this Learning Center, a list of new vocabulary words encountered in the unit readings should be kept and regularly updated. (See Section II for complete list.) Dictionaries and blank copies of the Vocabulary Web should be kept at the Center, as well as copies of student readings. Students visiting the Center may work alone or in small groups to develop Vocabulary Webs from unit vocabulary words, either compiling individual notebooks of webs or a class notebook. This Center allows students to gain more practice with the Vocabulary Web and to learn additional words, as class time will not allow all of the new words to be studied in depth.

b. **Language Study Center** (Lesson 4)

This Learning Center is intended to provide students with additional opportunities to study language. A set of task cards should be kept at the Center with short projects for students; they may keep a record in their notebooks of task card responses. Task cards may include several activities with different levels of difficulty, and points or scores may be assigned accordingly if the teacher so chooses. Some task cards may be activities students can complete on their own in the classroom, others might be small group activities, and others might require some work outside of class. Several sample task cards are listed below.

Card 1a. *The words "hear" and "here" sound the same but are spelled differently. These word pairs are called* **homophones** *or* **homonyms**. *Make a list of 20 different pairs of homophones. Can you think of a triple of homophones? A quadruple of homophones?*

Card 1b. *Complete a Vocabulary Web for the word* **homophone.**

Card 1c. *Use each pair of homophones in a single sentence.*

Card 1d. *Write silly sentences in which the meanings of two homophones are confused.*

Card 2a. *Look up the word "horrible" in three different dictionaries. How do the definitions compare? Did any of the dictionaries give additional information that was not given in the others?*

Card 2b. *Write a story in which you use the word "horrible" with each of the different meanings you found.*

Card 3. *Print the following sentence on a card:*

My cousins do not come to visit very often.

Ask at least 10 people to read it out loud. Notice how they say the word "often." Count how many pronounce the "t" and how many make it a silent "t." Check a dictionary for advice on pronunciation.

Card 4a. *In many words in the English language, we do not pronounce all of the letters we use to spell words. Write ten words which have a silent vowel and ten words which have a silent consonant.*

Card 4b. *See how many words you can write that have both a silent vowel and a silent consonant.*

Card 4c. *Put your "silent letter words" into categories. Can you see any patterns? Write a rule for each pattern that you see.*

Card 5a. *We have many different color words in our language. Make a chart of color words and find at least three different words for red, three for blue, and three for yellow.*

Card 5b. *Find the different color words in the dictionary and write explanations of how they are different.*

c. **Reading Center** (Lesson 4)

Short stories, poems, picture books, and chapter books may be made available at the Reading Center. These books may include those listed in the bibliography of extension readings as well as other materials. Students may keep a log of which pieces they have read, and may choose from a variety of assignments to complete based on their readings. Blank copies of the **Change Model** (Handout 2A) should be kept at this Center for students to fill in with examples from the stories that they read. Students may also write paragraphs to describe how the characters in a story changed or how the students themselves changed from reading the stories. New vocabulary words encountered in stories may be written in student notebooks for later exploration at the Vocabulary Web Center. The Reading Center may also serve as a small group discussion area in which students may talk about books they are reading with one another.

d. **Listening Center** (Lesson 4)

The Listening Center should have audio-taped books available for students, such as Joseph Bruchac's collection of Iroquois stories. As at the Reading Center, students should keep logs of what they hear, and may complete similar assignments to those listed above for the Reading Center. In addition, musical selections may be made available at the Listening Center. Question cards which emphasize the role of change in the music may be developed for these selections, including emphasis on how changes in the music can make the listener feel differently. Students may also write stories or poems based on the images created for them by the musical selections.

e. **Writing/Computer Center** (Lesson 5)

At this Learning Center, students have the opportunity to practice the stages of writing and the format of the persuasive paragraph. Writing materials and a word processing program should be made available to students, along with a list of suggested writing topics. Students may compose paragraphs and longer pieces at the Writing/ Computer Center, may work in pairs to critique one another's work, and may revise, edit, and publish their work. This Center may be used to work on unit assignments and/or on separate extension activities.

f. **Research Center** (Lesson 10)

This Learning Center may include a regular and an electronic encyclopedia, nonfiction books, and other resources which will help students in investigating their issue. A list of guiding questions and key terms to investigate may help students in their research efforts. In addition, this Center may include nonfiction materials about the authors whose works are included in the unit as well as the people, places, and things described in the readings, so that students may pursue areas of interest.

g. **Art/Writing Center** (Lesson 13)

This Center should contain a number of art cards which display prints of various artworks, including some of Escher's works. Students may use these cards as prompts for poetry or story writing or to answer questions about change (which may include completing a change model or answering specific questions listed on the art cards).

Use of Technology

Various elements of technology are used to enhance the effectiveness of the unit.

- ▼ A word processing program may be used for writing, revising, and editing written work. Students should be expected to use a spell checker to assist in the editing process.

- ▼ The research issue that is suggested in this unit, "What is the best way to preserve memories?" will generate much discussion of technologies such as videotape, various cameras, and computers.

The following information-gathering tools may be useful to students as they seek ideas and information. Teachers should ensure that students understand each information source and how to access it:

- ▼ CD-ROM library databases

- ▼ Interview or survey by electronic mail

- ▼ Specific resource materials on CD-ROM such as an encyclopedia, atlas, or other reference materials

- ▼ World Wide Web

Collaboration with Librarians

Because literature and information play key roles in the search for meaning, this unit depends on rich and extensive library resources. Working with librarians is essential for both teachers and students throughout the unit. Teachers and school librarians should work together in the planning stages of the unit to tailor the literature and research demands to the interests and abilities of the students. Because many of the resources suggested in this unit exceed the scope of school libraries, public and academic librarians should also be involved in the planning and implementation. Librarians can suggest resources, obtain materials on interlibrary loan, and work with students on research projects.

Students should be encouraged to become acquainted with the librarians in their community for several reasons. First, libraries are complex systems of organizing information. The systems vary from one library to another, and technological access to the systems is constantly changing. Librarians serve as expert guides to the information maze, and they are eager to assist library users. Secondly, the most important skill in using the library is knowing how to ask questions. Students should learn that working with a librarian is not a one-time inquiry or plea for assistance, but an interactive communication and discovery process. As the student asks a question and the librarian makes suggestions, the student will gain a better understanding of the topic and find new questions and ideas to explore. To exploit library resources fully, the student should then discuss these new questions and ideas with the librarian. Learning to use the services of librarians and other information professionals is an important tool for lifelong learning.

▼ Teaching Models

There are seven primary models that guided the development and initial teaching of the unit. These models are used consistently throughout the unit to ensure emphasis on unit outcomes. It is suggested that teachers become familiar with these models and how to implement them before using the unit. The models are listed below and outlined in the pages that follow.

1. The Taba Model of Concept Development
2. Literature Web Model
3. Vocabulary Web Model
4. Hamburger Model for Persuasive Writing
5. The Reasoning Model
6. The Writing Process Model
7. Research Model

The Concept Development Model

The concept development model, based upon the Hilda Taba Concept Development model (Taba, 1962), involves both inductive and deductive reasoning processes. Used as a beginning lesson in the unit (**Lesson 2**), the model focuses on the creation of generalizations from a student-derived list of created concepts. The model is comprised of seven steps and involves student participation at every step. Students begin with a broad concept, determine specific examples from that, create appropriate categorization systems, establish a generalization from those categories and then apply the generalization to their readings and other situations.

This model is best employed by dividing the class into small groups of 4–5 for initial work, followed by whole class discussion after each stage of the process.

1. Students generate examples of the concept of change, derived from students' own understanding and experiences with changes in the world. Teachers should encourage students to provide at least 25 examples.

2. Once an adequate number of examples have been elicited, students then group examples together into categories. Such a process allows students to search for interrelatedness, and to organize materials. Students should explain their reasoning for given categories and seek clarification from each other as a whole class. Teachers should ensure that students have accounted for all of their examples through the categories established.

3. Students are now asked to think of non-examples of the concept of change. Teachers may begin the brainstorming process with the direction, "Now list examples of things that *do not change.*" Teachers should encourage students to think carefully about non-examples and discuss ideas within their groups. Each group should list five to six examples.

4. The students now determine generalizations about the concept of change, using their lists of examples and nonexamples. Generalizations might include such ideas as "Change may be positive or negative" and "Change is linked to time." Generalizations should be derived from student input and may not precisely reflect the unit generalizations. Teachers should post the students' best generalizations on one side of the room and the prescribed unit generalizations on the other. Each set should be referred to throughout the unit.

5. Throughout the unit, students are asked to identify specific examples of the generalizations from their own readings, or to describe how the concept of change applies to a given situation about which they have read. Students are also asked to apply the generalizations to their own writings and their own lives.

Source: Taba, H. (1962). *Curriculum development: Theory and practice.* NY: Harcourt, Brace & World, Inc.

Practice webs using the generalizations about change are structured into core lessons in the unit. A change matrix, asking students to link ideas about change to literature used, is introduced in **Lesson 3** and revisited throughout the unit (**Lessons 10, 11, 15, 17, 19, 20, 21**), with a culminating activity in **Lesson 23**. A final assessment on how well students understand the concept of change may also be found in **Lesson 23**.

Note: The concept of change is discussed more fully in a paper to be found in the Appendix.

Literature Web Model

The Literature Web model encourages students to consider five aspects of a selection they are reading: key words (important, interesting, intriguing, surprising, or unknown to the reader), ideas, feelings (those of the reader), structure of writing (anything you notice about how the piece is written. For example, dialogue, rhyming, short sentences, or big words), and images (or symbols). The web helps students to organize their initial responses and provides them a platform for discussing the piece in small or large groups. Whenever possible, students should be allowed to underline and to make marginal notes as they read and reread. After marking the text, they then organize their notes into the web.

The Literature Web is introduced in **Lesson 3;** general steps for teaching the web are described below:

a. **Key Words:** Think and look back over the story. What were some words or groups of words that you really liked or thought were really important? Why were they special words to you? What were some words that you thought were interesting or exciting?

b. **Feelings:** What feelings did you get when you read the story? What feelings do you think the characters had? What happened in the story to tell you how the characters were feeling? Why do you think you had the feelings that you did?

c. **Ideas:** What was the main idea of the story? What were some of the other ideas the author was trying to talk about? What was she saying about change?

d. **Images:** What were some of the pictures that came to your mind as you read the story? What were some things about the story that may have had more than one meaning?

e. **Structure of Writing** (optional for this unit):* What were some important characteristics of the way this piece is put together? How does the rhyming pattern (dialogue, short sentences, etc.) contribute to the piece? How is the structure important for the meaning of the piece?

*Two versions of the Literature Web are included on the following pages. The Structure cell of the web has been removed for a primary adaptation of the model. Teachers should determine whether the primary adaptation of the complete model is more appropriate for their classes.

After students have completed their webs individually, they should compare their webs in small groups. This initial discussion will enable them to consider the ideas of others and to understand that individuals interpret literature differently. These small groups may compile a composite web that includes the ideas of all members.

Following the small group work, teachers have several options for using the webs. For instance, they may ask each group to report to the class; they may ask groups to post their composite webs; or they may develop a new web with the class based on the small group work. However, each web serves to prepare students to consider various issues the teacher will raise in whole group discussion. It is important that teachers hold a whole group discussion as the final aspect of implementing the model as a teaching-learning device. Teachers are encouraged to post the poem or story under consideration on an overhead or wherever it can be seen as the discussion is held. The teacher should record ideas, underline words listed, and call attention to student responses visually.

The Literature Web is employed in the following lessons:

▼ **Lesson 3**

▼ **Lesson 7**

▼ **Lesson 8**

▼ **Lesson 9**

▼ **Lesson 10**

▼ **Lesson 15**

▼ **Lesson 17**

▼ **Lesson 19**

▼ **Lesson 21**

▼ Literature Web Model

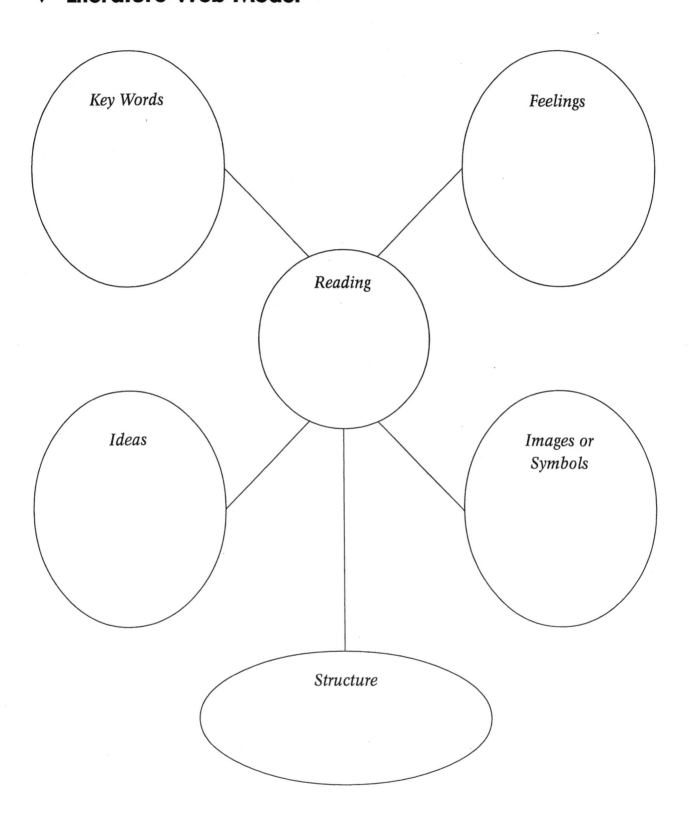

▼ Literature Web Model—Primary Adaptation

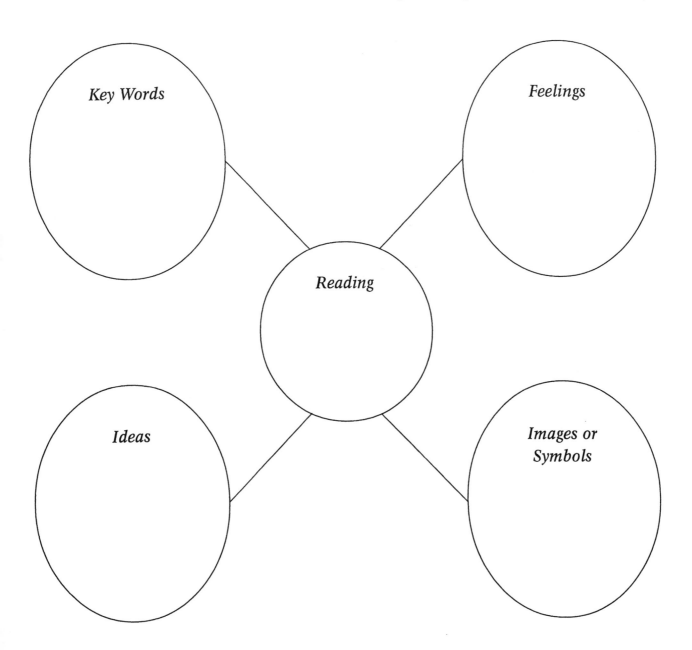

▼ Vocabulary Web Model

The purpose of the vocabulary web model is to enable students to grasp an in-depth understanding of interesting words. Rather than promoting superficial vocabulary development, the web approach allows for deep student processing of challenging and interesting words.

An example of a vocabulary web activity is given below. The teacher should introduce the activity by exploring the web with the whole class. This is introduced in **Lesson 4**; general steps are listed below, with the word *shepherd* as an example:

1. Introduce a **Vocabulary Web**. Put students in groups of no more than four, with a dictionary available as a resource in each group. Distribute copies of a blank Vocabulary Web and ask students to write the word *shepherd* in the center. Ask for an explanation of what the word means within the context of a given piece of literature. Have students find the word in the story and write the sentence in which it is found in the "Sentence" cell of the Vocabulary Web.

2. Ask students to look in their dictionaries to find the definition of the word. Display an enlarged copy of the definition on the board or overhead. Have students write the definition relevant to the story into the "Definition" cell of the Vocabulary Web.

3. Have students develop in their groups their own sentences using the word. Ask them to write the sentence in the "Example" cell.

4. Discuss the meanings of the words *synonym* and *antonym*. Have students check the dictionary and think about possible synonyms and antonyms for the word and fill them into the appropriate cells. (Note: Not all cells must be filled for all words; there may not be synonyms and antonyms for the words studied.)

5. Ask students what is meant by the phrase "part of speech." Have them locate the part of the dictionary definition that identifies a word's part of speech. Students should then write the part of speech for the word *shepherd* into their group webs.

6. Encourage students to think about the *stems* of the word, or the smaller words and pieces of words from which the larger word is made. These include prefixes, suffixes, and roots. Encourage students to check the dictionary for possible stems. Write any identified stems into the appropriate cell of the Vocabulary Web.

7. Have students locate the origin of the word (Latin, French, Greek, etc.) in the definition and write it in the *origin* cell of the Vocabulary Web.

8. Ask students to think of other words in the same family as the word *shepherd*, or other words which use one or more of the same stems. Encourage them to use their ideas from the stems cell to give them ideas.

9. Discuss the Vocabulary Webs developed by the student groups.

Note: Students may also add any number of extensions to the main circles if they identify additional information about the word.

Once students become familiar with this activity, they should use a streamlined version to accommodate new words they meet in their independent reading. A vocabulary section should be kept in a separate place in students' notebooks for this purpose. They need list only the word, definition, and sentence in which the word was encountered, plus any additional information they find particularly interesting. *The American Heritage Dictionary* (Third Edition) is recommended for this purpose.

The Vocabulary Web is employed in the following lessons of the unit:

▼ **Lesson 4**
▼ **Lesson 7**
▼ **Lesson 8**
▼ **Lesson 9**
▼ **Lesson 10**
▼ **Lesson 15**
▼ **Lesson 17**
▼ **Lesson 19**
▼ **Lesson 21**

▼ Vocabulary Web Model

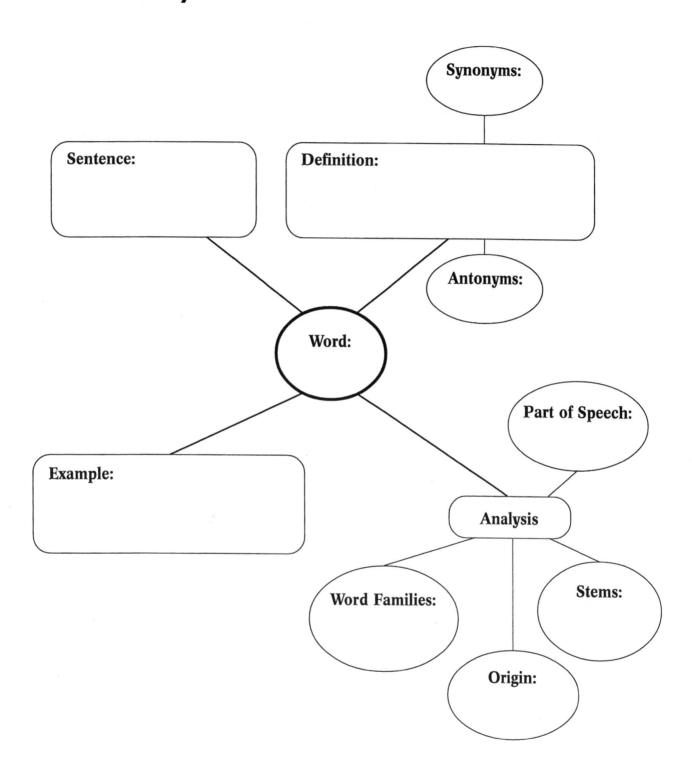

▼ The Hamburger Model for Persuasive Writing

The purpose of the Hamburger Model is to provide students with a useful metaphor to aid them in developing a persuasive paragraph or essay. The model should be introduced by the teacher, showing students that the top bun and the bottom bun represent the introduction and conclusion of any persuasive writing piece. The teacher should note that the reasons given in support of the thesis statement are like the meat or vegetables in a hamburger, providing the major substance of the sandwich. Elaboration represents the condiments in a sandwich, the ketchup, mustard, and onions that hold a sandwich together, just as examples and illustrations hold a persuasive writing piece together.

Teachers now should show students examples of hamburger paragraphs and essays (see **Lesson 5**) and have students find the top bun, bottom bun, hamburger, and condiments. Discuss how "good" each sandwich is.

Teachers may now ask students to construct their own "hamburger" paragraphs. After students have constructed their own hamburgers, teachers may use peer and self assessments to have students judge their own and one another's writing. This process should be repeated throughout the unit.

The Hamburger Model is addressed in the following lessons:

- ▼ **Lesson 5**
- ▼ **Lesson 6**
- ▼ **Lesson 8**
- ▼ **Lesson 9**
- ▼ **Lesson 10**
- ▼ **Lesson 11**
- ▼ **Lesson 12**
- ▼ **Lesson 13**
- ▼ **Lesson 18**
- ▼ **Lesson 22**
- ▼ **Lesson 23**
- ▼ **Lesson 24**

▼ Hamburger Model for Persuasive Writing

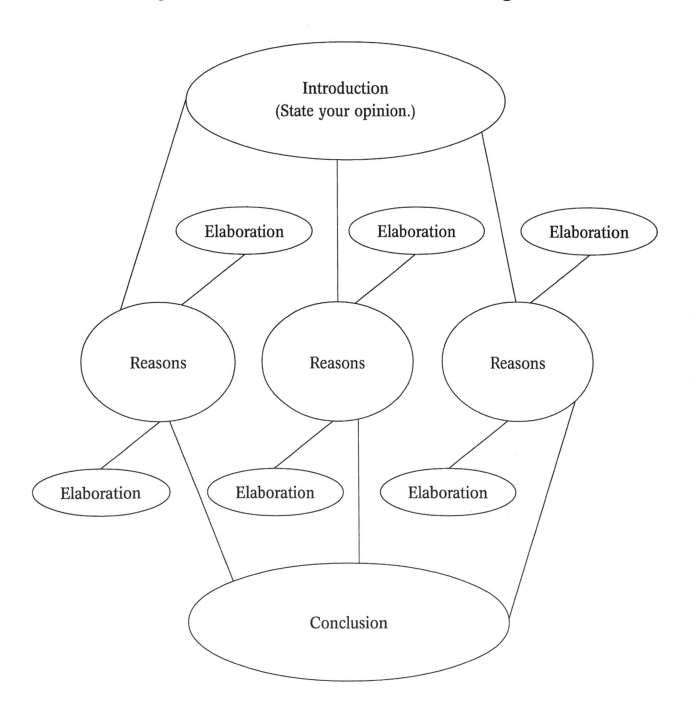

▼ The Writing Process Model

The writing process shows the stages that writers use to develop a written composition. The stages are not separate parts that writers go through from one to five; rather, writers move back and forth among the stages and use them to construct, clarify, and polish their writing. The writing process model is used throughout the unit to encourage students to engage in actively improving their own writing.

1. *Prewriting:* List your ideas and begin to organize them. You may want to use a graphic organizer such as a web or a Venn diagram. Graphic organizers help you to "see" what you will write about. As you write, you can add to your diagram or change it.

2. *Drafting:* Write a rough draft, getting your ideas onto paper and not worrying about mechanics such as spelling, grammar, or punctuation. Some writers call this stage "composing." Sometimes the first draft is a "messing around" stage in which your drafting or composing helps you to "hear" what you want to say.

3. *Revising:* Conferencing is an essential step in the revising stage. Ask people (friends, family, teachers) to read and listen to your work and to tell you what they like, what they don't understand, and what they'd like to know more about. This is the place to make major changes in your "composition" or draft. Sometimes you may want to go back to the prewriting stage and redo your organizer so that your paper has a new structure.

4. *Editing:* After you have revised your paper, look for the small changes that will make a big difference. Check your choice of words and identify mechanical errors. After you make the changes and corrections, proofread your work one final time. You may want to ask a friend or an adult for help.

5. *Sharing or Publishing:* There are numerous ways to share and to publish your work. You can bind it into a book, recopy it in your best handwriting and post it on a bulletin board, read it aloud to your class or family, or make it into a gift for someone special.

▼ Elements of Reasoning

The reasoning strand used throughout the unit focuses on eight elements identified by Richard Paul (1992). It is embedded in all lessons of the unit through questions, writing assignments, and research work. These elements of thought are the basic building blocks of productive thinking. Working together, they provide a general logic to reasoning. In literature interpretation and listening, they help one make sense of the reasoning of the author or speaker. In writing and speaking, they enable the author or speaker to strengthen their arguments.

Students are often asked to distinguish between facts and opinions. However, between pure opinion and hard facts lie reasoned judgments in which beliefs are supported by reasons. Instruction in this area needs to be included in all forms of communication in the language arts.

This unit is the first of a series of language arts units. All eight elements of reasoning are explained here, but not all of the elements will be used with students in this unit. Some will be added in succeeding units. Teachers may use these elements to assist in crafting questions for class discussion of literature or questions for probing student thinking. Examples of such questions are given on the wheel of reasoning that follows this page.

The eight elements of reasoning are as follows:

1. **Purpose, Goal, or End View:**

   We reason to achieve some objective, to satisfy a desire, to fulfill some need. For example, if the car does not start in the morning, the purpose of my reasoning is to figure out a way to get to work. One source of problems in reasoning is traceable to "defects" at the level of purpose or goal. If our goal itself is unrealistic, contradictory to other goals we have, confused or muddled in some way, then the reasoning we use to achieve it is problematic. If we are clear on the purpose for our writing and speaking, it will help focus the message in a coherent direction. The purpose in our reasoning might be to persuade others. When we read and listen, we should be able to determine the author's or speaker's purpose.

2. **Question at Issue (or Problem to Be Solved):**

   When we attempt to reason something out, there is at least one question at issue or problem to be solved (if not, there is no reasoning required). If we are not clear about what the question or problem is, it is unlikely that we will find a reasonable answer, or one that will serve our purpose. As part of the reasoning process, we should be able to formulate the question to be answered or the issue to be addressed. For example, why won't the car start? or should libraries censor materials that contain objectionable language?

3. **Points of View or Frame of Reference:**

   As we take on an issue, we are influenced by our own point of view. For example, parents of young children and librarians might have different points of view on censorship issues. The price of a shirt may seem low to one person while it seems high to another because of a different frame of reference. Any defect in our point of view or frame of reference is a possible source of problems in our reasoning. Our point of view may be too narrow, may not be precise enough, may be unfairly biased, and so forth. By considering multiple points of view, we may sharpen or broaden our thinking. In writing and speaking we may strengthen our arguments by acknowledging other points of view. In listening and reading, we need to identify the perspective of the speaker or author and understand how it affects the message delivered.

4. **Experiences, Data, Evidence:**

When we reason, we must be able to support our point of view with reasons or evidence. Evidence is important in order to distinguish opinions from reasons or to create a reasoned judgment. Evidence and data should support the author's or speaker's point of view and can strengthen an argument. An example is data from surveys or published studies. In reading and listening, we can evaluate the strength of an argument or the validity of a statement by examining the supporting data or evidence. Experiences can also contribute to the data of our reasoning. For example, previous experiences in trying to get a car to start, may contribute to the reasoning process that is necessary to resolve the problem.

5. **Concepts and Ideas:**

Reasoning requires the understanding and use of concepts and ideas (including definitional terms, principles, rules, or theories). When we read and listen, we can ask ourselves, "What are the key ideas presented?" When we write and speak, we can examine and organize our thoughts around the substance of concepts and ideas. Some examples of concepts are freedom, friendship, and responsibility.

6. **Assumptions:**

We need to take some things for granted when we reason. We need to be aware of the assumptions we have made and the assumptions of others. If we make faulty assumptions, this can lead to defects in reasoning. As a writer or speaker we make assumptions about our audience and our message. For example, we might assume that others will share our point of view; or we might assume that the audience is familiar with the First Amendment when we refer to "First Amendment rights." As a reader or listener we should be able to identify the assumptions of the writer or speaker.

7. **Inferences:**

Reasoning proceeds by steps call inferences. An inference is a small step of the mind, in which a person concludes that something is so because of something else being so or seeming to be so. The tentative conclusions (inferences) we make depend on what we assume as we attempt to make sense of what is going on around us. For example, we see dark clouds and infer that it is going to rain; or we know the movie starts at 7:00; it is now 6:45: it takes 30 minutes to get to the theater; so we cannot get there on time. Many of our inferences are justified and reasonable, but many are not. We need to distinguish between the raw data of our experiences and our interpretations of those experiences (inferences). Also the inferences we make are heavily influenced by our point of view and our assumptions.

8. **Implications and Consequences:**

When we reason in a certain direction, we need to look at the consequences of that direction. When we argue and support a certain point of view, solid reasoning requires that we consider what the implications are of following that path; what are the consequences of taking the course that we support? When we read or listen to an argument, we need to ask ourselves what follows from that way of thinking. We can also consider consequences of actions that characters in stories take. For example, if I don't do my homework, I will have to stay after school to do it; or if I water the lawn, it will not wither in the summer heat.

Adapted from Paul, R. (1992). *Critical thinking: What every person needs to survive in a rapidly changing world*. CA: Foundation for Critical Thinking.

▼ Wheel of Reasoning

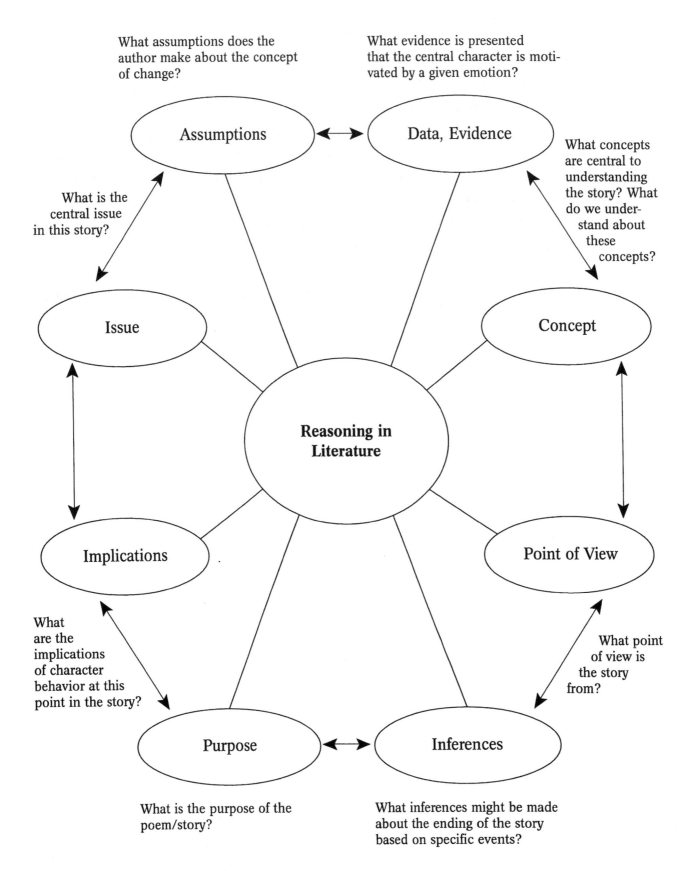

What assumptions does the author make about the concept of change?

What evidence is presented that the central character is motivated by a given emotion?

Assumptions

Data, Evidence

What concepts are central to understanding the story? What do we understand about these concepts?

What is the central issue in this story?

Issue

Concept

Reasoning in Literature

Implications

Point of View

What are the implications of character behavior at this point in the story?

Purpose

Inferences

What point of view is the story from?

What is the purpose of the poem/story?

What inferences might be made about the ending of the story based on specific events?

▼ Research Model

The research model provides students a way to approach an issue of significance and explore it individually and in small groups. Its organization follows major elements of reasoning. Teachers are encouraged to model each stage of this process in class. For specific lessons in teaching the research model, procure a copy of *A Guide to Teaching Research Skills and Strategies in Grades 4–12*, available from the Center for Gifted Education at The College of William and Mary.

---

1. **Identify your issue or problem.**

What is the issue or problem?

Who are the stakeholders and what are their positions?

What is *your* position on this issue?

---

2. **Read about your issue and identify points of view or arguments through information sources.**

What are my print sources?

What are my media sources?

What are my people sources?

What are my preliminary findings based on a review of existing sources?

---

3. **Form a set of questions that can be answered by people you would like to interview who understand the issue or problem.**

My Interview Questions:

4. Organize evidence and data gathered through interviews and other information sources by using 3x5 cards to record information from each source.

What did I find out from each source?

Which of my questions have been answered by which sources?

What are some ideas which I found in more than one source?

What are some issues about which my sources disagreed?

5. Prepare a report based on your ordered cards. Remember to answer all of the following questions in your report.

What is the issue or problem?

What different perspectives are taken on the issue?

What is your position?

What data or evidence support your position?

What conclusions do you make about your issue?

What consequences do you see of your position?

6. Communicate your findings. (Prepare an oral presentation for classmates based on note cards and written report.)

What are my purpose, issue, and point of view, and how will I explain them?

What data will I use to support my point of view?

How will I conclude my presentation?

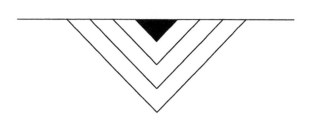

SECTION

IV

BIBLIOGRAPHIES

This section includes two bibliographies of works used in the unit and additional resources. The first bibliography lists student readings employed directly in the unit or referenced in extension activities. The second bibliography lists teacher resources.

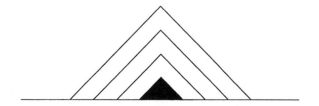

▼ Bibliography of Student Readings

Aardema, V. (1960). *What's so funny, Ketu? A Nuer tale*. New York: Dial.

Aardema, V. (1981). *Bringing the rain to Kapiti plain*. New York: Dial.

Aardema, V. (1984). *Oh, Kojo! How could you!* New York: Dial.

Aardema, V. (1984). *Who's in Rabbit's house?* New York: Dial.

Aardema, V. (1984). *Why mosquitoes buzz in people's ears*. New York: Dial.

Aardema, V. (1985). *Bimwili and the Zimwi*. New York: Dial.

Aesop for children. (1984). Chicago: Rand McNally.

Andersen, H. C. (1959). *Seven tales by H. C. Andersen* (E. Le Gallienne, Trans.). New York: Harper & Row.

Andersen, H. C. (1965). *The nightingale* (E. Le Gallienne, Trans.). New York: Harper & Row.

Andersen, H. C. (1978). *Hans Andersen: His classic fairy tales* (E. Haugaard, Trans.). New York: Doubleday.

Andersen, H. C. (1981). *The wild swans* (A. Ehrlich, Retold). New York: Dial.

Andersen, H. C. (1985). *The nightingale* (A. Bell, Trans.). New York: Picture Book Studio.

Andersen, H. C. (1985). *The nightingale* (A. Bier, Adapted). New York: Harcourt Brace Jovanovich.

Anno, M. (1977). *Anno's journey*. New York: HarperCollins.

Briggs, R. (1978). *The snowman*. New York: Random House.

Bruchac, J. (1988). *Iroquois stories*. New York: Good Mind Records.

Bunting, E. (1982). *The happy funeral*. New York: HarperCollins.

Burrows, W. E. (1993). *Mission to deep space: Voyager's journey of discovery*. New York: W.H. Freeman.

Byars, B. (1968). *The midnight fox*. New York: Viking.

Byars, B. (1986). *The not-just-anybody family*. New York: Dell Yearling.

Byars, B. (1987). *The blossoms and the green phantom*. New York: Delacorte.

Cooney, B. (1982). *Miss Rumphius*. New York: Viking.

Coutant, H. (1974). *First snow*. New York: Knopf.

Dickinson, E. (1978). *I'm nobody! Who are you? Poems of Emily Dickinson for young people*. Owings Mills, MD: Stemmer House.

Friedman, I. R. (1984). *How my parents learned to eat*. New York: Houghton Mifflin.

Greenfield, E. (1988). *Grandpa's face*. New York: Putnam.

Greenfield, E. (1989). *Nathaniel talking*. New York: Black Butterfly.

Haley, G. E. (1977). *Go away, stay away*. New York: Scribner's.

Haley, G. E. (1984). *Birdsong*. New York: Crown.

Haley, G. E. (1986). *Jack and the bean tree*. New York: Crown.

Haley, G. E. (1988). *Jack and the fire dragon*. New York: Crown.

Haley, G. E. (1988). *The green man*. Blowing Rock, NC: New River.

Haugaard, E. (1978). *Hans Andersen: His classic fairy tales*. New York: Doubleday.

Holdridge, B. (Ed.) (1986). *Under the greenwood tree*. Owings Mills, MD: Stemmer House.

Hopkins, L. (1986). *Best friends*. New York: Harper and Row.

Jarrell, R. (1963). *The bat-poet*. New York: Macmillan.

Lord, B. B. (1984). *In the year of the boar and Jackie Robinson*. New York: HarperCollins.

O'Neill, M. (1989). *Hailstones and halibut bones*. New York: Doubleday.

Pinkwater, D. M. (1977). *The big orange splot*. New York: Hastings.

Pyle, H. (1909). *The adventures of Robin Hood*. New York: Scribner.

Reimer, L., & Reimer, W. (1990). *Mathematicians are people, too*. Palo Alto, CA: Dale Seymour.

Rylant, C. (1983). *Miss Maggie*. New York: Dutton.

Rylant, C. (1985). *Every living thing*. New York: Aladdin.

Rylant, C. (1985). *The relatives came*. New York: Bradbury.

Rylant, C. (1988). *All I see*. New York: Orchard.

Rylant, C. (1991). *Appalachia: The voices of sleeping birds*. San Diego: Harcourt Brace Jovanovich.

Rylant, C. (1992). *An angel for Solomon Singer*. New York: Orchard.

Sakai, K. (1990). *Sachiko means happiness*. San Francisco: Children's Book Press.

Stanley, D., & Vennema, P. (1992). *Bard of Avon*. New York: Morrow Junior Books.

Stock, C. (1984). *Emma's dragon hunt*. New York: Lothrop, Lee, & Shepard.

Tolan, S. (1983). *A time to fly free*. New York: Scribner.

Van Allsburg, C. V. (1984). *The mysteries of Harris Burdick*. Boston: Houghton Mifflin.

Walsh, J. P. (1982). *The green book*. New York: Farrar Straus Giroux.

Wiesner, D. (1988). *Free fall*. New York: Lothrop, Lee, & Shepard.

Williams, V. B. (1986). *Cherries and cherry pits*. New York: Greenwillow.

Wisniewski, D. (1991) *Rain player*. New York: Clarion.

▼ Bibliography of Teacher Resources

American heritage dictionary of the English language. (3rd. ed). (1992). Boston: Houghton-Mifflin.

Appel, A., Jr. (1992). *The art of celebration: Twentieth-century painting, literature, sculpture, photography, and jazz*. New York: Alfred A. Knopf.

Baskin, B. H., & Harris, K. H. (1980). *Books for the gifted child*. New York: Bowker.

Costa, A. L. (Ed.) (1991). *Developing minds*. (Rev. ed., Vol. 1–2). Alexandria, VA: Association for Supervision and Curriculum Development.

Dallas Museum of Art. (1989). *Ancestral legacy: The African impulse in African-American art*. Dallas, TX: Author.

Derwin, S., & Mills, C. (1988). *Introduction to the classics*. Baltimore, MD: Johns Hopkins University, Center for Talented Youth.

Escher, M. C. (1967). *The graphic work of M. C. Escher* (rev. ed.). New York: Ballantine.

Escher, M. C. (1974). *The graphic work of M. C. Escher* (8th ed.). New York: Ballantine.

Feder, N. (1965). *American Indian art*. New York: Harry N. Abrams.

Frank, M. (1987). *Complete writing lessons for the middle grades*. Nashville, TN: Incentive Publication.

Furst, P. T., & Furst, J. L. (1982). *North American Indian art*. New York: Rizzoli.

Great Books Foundation. (1992). *An introduction to shared inquiry* (3rd. ed.). Chicago: Author.

Halsted, J. W. (1988). *Guiding gifted readers: From preschool through high school*. Columbus, OH: Ohio Psychology Press.

Harris, V. J. (Ed.) (1992). *Teaching multicultural literature in grades K–8*. Norwood, MA: Christopher-Gordon.

Hauser, P., & Nelson, G. A. (1988). *Books for the gifted child, volume 2*. New York: Bowker.

Henderson, K. (1988). *Market guide for young writers*. Belvidere, NJ: Shoe Tree Press.

Highwater, J. (1978). *Many smokes, many moons: A chronology of American Indian history through Indian art*. Philadelphia, PA: J. B. Lippincott.

Highwater, J. (1983). *Arts of the Indian Americans: Leaves from the sacred tree*. New York: Harper & Row.

Koch, K., & Farrell, K. (1985). *Talking to the sun: An illustrated anthology of poems for young people*. New York: Metropolitan Museum of Art and Henry Holt.

Levine, E. (1989). *I hate English!* New York: Scholastic.

Marzano, R. J. (1992). *Cultivating thinking in English*. Urbana, IL: National Council of Teachers of English.

Marzano, R. J., Pickering, D. J., Arrendondo, D. E., Blackburn, G. J., Brandt, R. S., & Moffett, C. A. (1992). *Dimensions of learning: Teacher's manual*. Alexandria, VA: Association for Supervision and Curriculum Development.

Miller-Lachmann, L. (1992). *Our family, our friends, our world: An annotated guide to significant multicultural books for children and teenagers*. New Providence, NJ: Bowker.

National Assessment Examining Board. (1992). *Exploring new methods for collecting students' school-based writing: NAEP's portfolio study*. Washington, DC: U. S. Government Printing Office.

National Assessment Examining Board. (1992). *Reading framework for the 1992 National Assessment of Educational Progress*. Washington, DC: U. S. Government Printing Office.

The National Museum of Women in the Arts. (1987). *Women in the arts*. New York: Harry N. Abrams.

Novak, J. D., & Gowin, D. B. (1984). *Learning how to learn*. New York: Cambridge University Press.

Paul, R. (1992). *Critical thinking: What every person needs to survive in a rapidly changing world*. CA: The Foundation for Critical Thinking.

Paul, R., Binker, A. J. A., Jensen, K., & Kreklau, H. (1990). *Critical thinking handbook: 4th–6th grades, a guide for remodeling lesson plans in language arts, social studies, and science*. Rohnert Park, CA: Sonoma State University, Foundation for Critical Thinking.

Purves, A. C., Rogers, T., & Soter, A. O. (1990). *How porcupines make love II: Teaching a response-centered literature curriculum*. New York: Longman.

Ravitch, D. (Ed.) (1990). *The American reader: Words that moved a nation*. New York: HarperCollins.

Sullivan, C. (Ed.). (1989). *Imaginary gardens: American poetry and art for young people*. New York: Harry N. Abrams.

Sullivan, C. (Ed.) (1991). *Children of promise: African-American literature and art for young people*. New York: Harry N. Abrams.

Taba, H. (1962). *Curriculum development: Theory and practice*. New York: Harcourt, Brace & World.

Tchudi, S. (1991). *Planning and assessing the curriculum in English language arts*. Alexandria, VA: Association for Supervision and Curriculum Development.

Thompson, M. C. (1990). *Classics in the classroom*. Monroe, New York: Trillium.

Thompson, M. C. (1990–1991). *The word within the word* (Vols. 1 & 2). Unionville, New York: Trillium.

Thompson, M. C. (1991). *The magic lens: A spiral tour through the human ideas of grammar.* Unionville, NY: Trillium.

UNICEF Ontario Development Education Committee. (1988). *Children's literature: Springboard to understanding the developing world.* Canada: Canadian International Development Agency.

VanTassel-Baska, J., Johnson, D. T., & Boyce, L. N. (Eds.) (1996). *Developing verbal talent.* Boston: Allyn & Bacon.

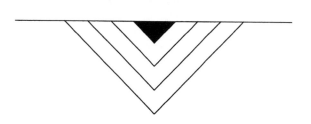

APPENDIX

THE CONCEPT OF CHANGE

This unit is organized around the concept of change and how it functions in litera-ture, writing, speech, and language. As a theme in literature, it is viewed at the level of character growth and development over time and at the levels of social and cultural change which are apparent in literary contexts.

Teachers are encouraged to read the following paper as a prelude to teaching the concept of change. The paper provides a broad-based background in understanding the concept and additional readings for further understanding.

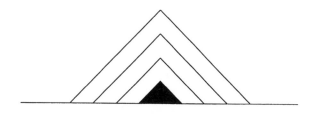

▼ The Concept of Change: Interdisciplinary Inquiry and Meaning

by Linda Neal Boyce

What Is Change?

Because change is a complex concept that inspires fear as well as hope, the idea of change has engaged thinkers throughout the ages and across disciplines. Change is therefore best studied as an interdisciplinary concept for several reasons. First, an understanding of change in one discipline informs the study of change in another discipline and results in important connections. Secondly, an interdisciplinary study of change provides insights into the structure of each discipline. Equally important, the increasing rate of global change resulting in social, political, and environmental upheaval, an information explosion, and a technological revolution creates an urgent need to understand the dynamics of change.

To provide a basis for understanding change as a concept, this paper explores change in several disciplines. While exploring the concepts, it identifies resources for teachers and for students that focus on change. Finally, the paper examines the way the concept of change was applied in the National Language Arts Project for High Ability Learners.

Religion and Philosophy

The *Encyclopedia of Philosophy* (Capek, 1967) and *Encyclopedia of Religion and Ethics* (Hyslop, 1910) provide overviews of change from the perspectives of religion and philosophy. Both sources agree that change is one of the most basic and pervasive features of our experience. Hyslop goes so far as to say that change is difficult to define and that it is easier to discuss the types of change. He identifies four types of change: (1) qualitative change, a change in the qualities or properties of a subject such as chemical reaction; (2) quantitative change which includes expansion, contraction, detrition, and accretion; (3) local change, or a change in the subject's position in space; and (4) formal change, a change of shape. He adds that all changes involve time which is an essential condition of change.

Historically, philosophers and theologians have not always acknowledged the existence of change (Capek, 1967; Hyslop, 1910). Ideas of God, Being, and One that are based on eternal order and perfection of nature regard time and change as illusions of finite experience. Hyslop points out that acknowledging change is crucial to inquiry; that change represents the dynamic as the source of all investigations into causes. He states, "Curiosity regarding causal agency begins with the discovery of change and terminates in explanation" (p. 357). Capek's and Hyslop's essays offer an important backdrop to our understanding of the current controversies, the intense emotion, and the values that surround the concept of change.

Social Studies

In his outline of "Social Studies within a Global Education," Kniep (1989/1991) identifies change as one of the conceptual themes for social studies and asserts, "The process of movement from one state of being to another is a universal aspect of the planet and is an inevitable part of life and living" (p. 121). He lists adaptation, cause and effect, development, evolution, growth, revolution, and time as related concepts. Kniep's comprehensive scope and sequence for social studies includes: (1) essential elements (systems, human values, persistent issues and problems, and global history); (2) conceptual themes (interdependence, change, culture, scarcity, and conflict); (3) phenomenological themes (people, places, and events), and (4) persistent problem themes (peace and security, national/international development, environmental problems, and human rights). Change is both a concept to understand and an agent to consider in all social studies ideas and themes.

In discussing social change, Daniel Chirot (1985) views social change as pervasive. He states that most societies, however, delude themselves into believing that stability prevails and that unchanging norms can be a reality.

Chirot identifies demographic change, technological change, and political change as the most important causes of general social change. In his discussion of how and why critical changes have occurred, Chirot considers three transformations in social structure among the most important:

▼ The technological revolution produced by the adoption of sedentary agriculture

▼ The organizational revolution that accompanied the rise of states

▼ The current "modernization" that encompasses major changes in thought, technology, and politics (p. 761).

He points out that studying current major changes such as the increasing power of the state and the proletarianization of labor helps us understand smaller changes such as those in family structure, local political organizations, types of protest, and work habits. Because change impacts on our lives in large and small ways, we must understand and confront it.

Vogt's (1968) analysis of cultural change echoes Chirot's discussion of social change: "It can now be demonstrated from our accumulated archeological and historical data that a culture is never static, but rather that one of its most fundamental properties is change" (p. 556). Vogt cites three factors that influence change in a given culture:

▼ Any change in the ecological niche as a result of natural environmental changes or the migration of a society as when the Anasazi Indians left Mesa Verde to find new homes and lost their cultural identity in the process

▼ Any contact between two societies with different cultural patterns as when Hispanic and Native American cultures converged in New Mexico

▼ Any evolutionary change occurring within a society such as when a food-gathering society domesticates its plants and animals or incorporates technology to effect lifestyle changes.

In his discussion of cultural adaptation, Carneiro (1968) distinguishes between cultural adaptation (the adjustment of a society to its external and internal conditions) and cultural evolution (change by which a society grows complex and better integrated). Adaptation may include simplification and loss resulting from a deteriorating environment. Thus, adaptation may signal negative as well as positive changes for a cultural group.

History—the social sciences discipline that chronicles change—provides insight into specific changes from a range of perspectives. For instance, resources such as *The Timetables of History* (Grun, 1991) and the *Smithsonian Timelines of the Ancient World* (Scarre, 1993) record changes by significant annual events in the areas of history and politics; literature and theater; religion, philosophy, and learning; the visual arts; music; science and technology; and daily life. These tools allow readers to see at a glance the simultaneous events and significant people involved in changes occurring throughout the world or in a specific area.

Various scholars chronicle ideas about change on an interdisciplinary canvas. Boorstin (1983) focuses on man's need to know and the courage of those who challenged dogma at various times in history. He provides an in-depth look at the causes of change, considering such questions as why the Chinese did not "discover" Europe and America and why the Egyptians and not the Greeks invented the calendar. Tamplin (1991) demonstrates the interrelationship of personal, cultural, and societal change with discussions and illustrations of literature, visual arts, architecture, music, and the performing arts. Petroski (1992) chronicles change and investigates its origins through technology. He argues that shortcomings are the driving force for change and sees inventors as critics who have a compelling urge to tinker with things and to improve them.

Science

Echoing the call for curriculum reform that centers on an in-depth study of broad concepts, Rutherford and Ahlgren (1979) in *Science for All Americans* state:

> Some important themes pervade science, mathematics, and technology and appear over and over again, whether we are looking at an ancient civilization, the human body, or a comet. They are ideas that transcend disciplinary boundaries and prove fruitful in explanation, in theory, in observation, and in design.

Rutherford and Ahlgren proceed to recommend six themes: systems, models, constancy, patterns of change, evolution, and scale. Of the six themes, three of them—constancy, patterns of change, and evolution—focus on change or its inverse. In discussing patterns of change, Rutherford and Ahlgren identify three general categories, all of which have applicability in other disciplines: (1) changes that are steady trends, (2) changes that occur in cycles, and (3) changes that are irregular.

Sher (1993) identifies and discusses four general patterns of change: (1) steady changes: those that occur at a characteristic rate; (2) cyclic changes: those changes that repeat in cycles; (3) random changes: those changes that occur irregularly, unpredictably, and in a way that is mathematically random; and (4) chaotic change: change that appears random and irregular on the surface, but is in fact or principle predictable. She considers the understanding of chaotic change as one of the most exciting developments in recent science.

As in the other disciplines, change in science can be studied as a concept and as a specific application or type of change. For example, our view of the earth over the last 40 years has changed from a static globe model to a dynamic plate tectonics model, affecting our understanding of earthquakes, volcanoes, and other seismic events (NASA, 1988; 1990).

Language—Creative and Changing

S. I. and Alan Hayakawa in *Language in Thought and Action* (1990) state categorically, "Language . . . makes progress possible" (p. 7). They argue that reading and writing make it possible to pool experience and that "cultural and intellectual cooperation is, or should be, the great principle of human life" (p. 8). They then examine the relationships among language, thought, and behavior and how language changes thinking and behavior. For instance, they discuss how judgments stop thought therefore leading to unfounded and dangerous generalizations. They explore the changing meanings of words and point out "no word ever has exactly the same meaning twice" (p. 39). For the Hayakawas, dictionaries are not authoritative statements about words but rather historical records of the meanings of words. Finally, the Hayakawas discuss the paralyzing effects of fear of change and the anger that accompanies it. They propose that the debate around issues facing society should center on specific questions such as "What will be the results?" "Who would benefit, and by how much?" and "Who would be harmed, and to what degree?" rather than questions of "right" or "wrong." They contend that this way of thinking reflects a scientific attitude and harnesses language to accurately "map" social and individual problems, thereby enabling change.

While *Language in Thought and Action* is an eloquent manifesto about the possibilities of language, the anthology *Language Awareness* (Eschholz, Rosa, & Clark, 1982) provides a resource on specific topics. The essays cover the history of language, language in politics and propaganda; the language of advertising; media and language, jargon, names, prejudice and language; taboos and euphemisms; language play; and the responsible use of language. Each essay examines either changes in language or how language changes thinking and action. For example, in her outline of the devices of propaganda that include name calling, generalities, "plain folks" appeal, stroking, personal attacks, guilt or glory by association, bandwagon appeals, faulty cause and effect, false analogy, and testimonials, Cross (1982) examines the manipulative power of language.

The powers of language range from strident manipulation to the quiet heightening of awareness. Response to language involves a change—a change of perspective, a new understanding, an insight in the search for meaning. Coles (1989) speaks of the power of literature to give direction to life and to awaken moral sensibilities. He states, "Novels and stories are renderings of life; they cannot only keep us company, but admonish us, point us in new directions, or give us the courage to stay a given course" (p. 159).

While Coles discusses the impact of literature on private lives, Downs (1978) discusses revolutionary books throughout history in his *Books That Changed the World*. Examining such books as *The Bible*, Machiavelli's *The Prince*, Beecher's *Uncle Tom's Cabin*, Darwin's *Origin of Species*, and Freud's *The Interpretation of Dreams*, Downs attempts to discover and to analyze two categories of writings: works that were direct, immediate instruments in determining the course of events, and works that molded minds over centuries. He concludes that, "Omitting the scientists in the group, for whom these comments are less pertinent, the books [which changed the world] printed since 1500 were written by nonconformists, radicals, fanatics, revolutionists, and agitators" (p. 25).

The reading process which enables readers to search for information and meaning is an active, recursive process that includes choosing a book, reading, discussing from the reader's point of view, listening to another's point of view, reflecting and responding, and re-reading or making a new choice (Bailey, Boyce, VanTassel-Baska, 1990). Effective reading includes revising an interpretation or changing ideas, a step which is mirrored in the writing process and in speaking and listening. Kennedy (1993) sees all of the language processes—reading, writing, speaking, listening, and thinking—as complex, interrelated activities; activities that result in a dynamic, changing discourse.

Censorship reflects the public's acknowledgment and fear of the power of language to change thinking, behavior, and society at large. The debate over censorship and freedom of expression has raged for centuries and ranges from the use of racist and sexist language in literature to the effects of violence on television. Plato, one may remember, argued against allowing children to listen to imaginative stories and banned the poets from his ideal society. The continuing controversy regarding the burning of the American flag is one of several censorship issues widely debated in our society that illustrates the linkage of symbols, language, and freedom of expression (Bradbury and Quinn, 1991).

Telecommunications in a Changing World

Telecommunications has dramatically changed our capacity to access information. Electronic mail, known as e-mail, is a telecommunications system that links computers around the world through telephone lines and satellites. It has created significant changes in scientific and business communities such as: increased flexibility for team members working in various locations across time zones, an end to isolation of researchers around the world, and the restructuring of organizations by eliminating corporate hierarchies (Perry, 1992a). Perry also cites the role of e-mail in the Russian coup of Boris Yeltsin and the use of faxes during the Tiananmen uprising. E-mail and fax machines provided sources of information that were difficult to control and allowed dissenters to communicate with one another and with the outside world (Perry, 1992b).

Video, television, cable, compact discs, and computers and the Internet are transforming not only access to information, but the content of information as well. In a recent *U.S. News and World Report* article John Leo (March 8, 1993) discusses the new standard of television news that blends information and entertainment. He contends that images, story line, and emotional impact are replacing a commitment to evidence, ethics, and truth. In another development, compact discs and computers are combining sound tracks, animation, photography, and print information that replace standard multi-volume encyclopedias and that enable users to combine information in new ways. The Grolier Multimedia Encyclopedia (1994) on CD-ROM for example, supplements its text with features such as animated multimedia maps that show the growth and development of American railroads, the women's suffrage movement, and other topics. This changing information technology demands new standards for the evaluation of information and new consideration of how technology can limit or expand thinking.

The Concept of Change and Language Arts Unit Development

For the purposes of teaching the concept of change for the National Javits Language Arts Project for High Ability Learners, five generalizations about change were drawn from the literature of various disciplines. Table I illustrates those generalizations and their accompanying outcomes. Examples of how the generalizations were addressed in the units through language study, language processes, and literature follow Table I.

Language Study

Throughout the units, word study and vocabulary served as a primary source for studying change. Students constructed vocabulary webs that mapped words by (1) the definition; (2) a sentence that used the word from the literature being studied; (3) an example of the word; and (4) an analysis of the word that identified stems (roots, prefixes, and suffixes), word families, and word history. To build on the verbal talent of high ability learners, resources such as *Sumer is Icumen In: Our Ever-Changing Language* by Greenfeld (1978) and *Oxford Guide to Word Games* by Augarde (1984) were included in the units to encourage students to explore language changes and to play with the possibilities of inventing it themselves.

Each unit included a grammar packet developed by Michael Thompson and based on his work, *The Magic Lens: A Spiral Tour through the Human Ideas of Grammar* (1991). Thompson's packets were designed to help students learn why some ideas are clear and others are confusing; to understand the power of grammar to reveal deep thinking and deep

▼ Table I
Generalizations and Outcomes about Change

Generalizations	Outcomes
1. Change is pervasive.	Understand that change permeates our lives and our universe.
2. Change is linked to time.	Illustrate the variability of change based on time.
3. Change may be perceived as systematic or random.	Categorize types of change, given several examples. Demonstrate the change process at work in a piece of literature.
4. Change may represent growth and development or regression and decay.	Interpret change in selected works as progressive or regressive.
5. Change may occur according to natural order or be imposed by individuals or groups.	Analyze social and individual change in a given piece of literature.

meaning. Implicit in this study was the idea that changing the grammar of a sentence or paragraph meant changing its meaning. Literature selections upon which the units were built and the students' own writing provided the context for studying grammar.

Language Processes

The processes of reading, writing, listening, and speaking were studied as change processes. Literature discussions were based on the premise that each person's interpretation and understanding of meaning would be different from another person's interpretation. Through listening to one another, students were encouraged to seek new meaning and to examine how their interpretations changed during the discussion. In like manner, students studied the writing process as a way to explore ideas and to generate their own thinking and learning. The revision stage of writing emphasized seeking feedback and listening to responses from teachers and peers. Considering another's perspective often led to changes in the understanding of one's own work and to subsequent changes in the structure and clarity of the writing.

Oral communications in these units centered on persuasive speaking and critical listening. Students studied how to change their audience's opinion and actions through argument formulation and strategies of persuasion. As students listened to persuasive speeches, they analyzed the arguments and evaluated their effectiveness. Resources for the speaking and listening components included videotapes of master persuaders such as Franklin D. Roosevelt, Martin Luther King, Jr., and Adolph Hitler that provided students with opportunities to consider the role of persuasion in social and historical contexts. Other resources such as *The American Reader: Words That Moved a Nation* (Ravitch, 1990) documented the persuasive role of oral communications such as orations, Congressional hearings, and songs in the process of change.

Literature

Each of the units was developed around literature selections with vocabulary and language study emerging from the selections. The development of the concept of change also emerged from the literature discussions and activities. Typically each literary piece was examined for evidence of character changes, both physical and psychological, as well as social, political, and economic changes. For instance in "The Power of Light" by I. B. Singer (1962) students discussed the issue of whether characters change themselves or are changed by events outside of their control.

In addition to the literature selections which were discussed with the total group, additional resources embedded in each unit illustrated the generalizations about change and addressed the social, cultural and environmental implications of change. For instance, *Commodore Perry in the Land of the Shogun* (Blumberg, 1985) documents the dramatic social and cultural changes created by Perry's visits to Japan in 1853 and 1854. Illustrated with reproductions of primary sources, the account presents misconceptions, hostilities, and humorous episodes encountered from multiple points of view. Change is palpable while reading the book. A very different book, *Letting Swift River Go* by Yolen (1992) tells of the drowning of a Swift River town for the building of the Quabbin Reservoir, a water supply for Boston and now a wilderness area. The open-ended story alludes to necessary tradeoffs and provides opportunities to discuss changes linked to time as well as the positive and negative aspects of change.

Conclusion

The idea of change crosses all disciplines and offers learners an opportunity to construct a concept that will inform their lives in meaningful ways. Because of the accelerating rate of change in our world, students need to understand the concept and to acquire effective tools for meeting its challenges. Language with its powers of inquiry, persuasion, and critique provides a powerful tool for meeting the challenges of change.

Literature, in particular, offers students and teachers a rich content arena for analyzing change and for considering the issues that surround it. Literature captures the voices, the emotions, and the concerns of thinkers through the ages and across cultures. It demonstrates types of change, responses to change, the causes and agents of change, as well as the effects of change. In a time of dizzying change, literature also offers continuity and a welcomed opportunity for reflection.

▼ References

Augarde, T. (1984). *The Oxford guide to word games.* Oxford: Oxford University Press.

Bailey, J. M., Boyce, L. N., & VanTassel-Baska, J. (1990). The writing, reading, and counseling connection: A framework for serving the gifted. In J. VanTassel-Baska (Ed.), *A practical guide to counseling the gifted in a school setting* (2d ed.) (pp. 72–89). Reston, VA: The Council for Exceptional Children.

Blumberg, R. (1985). *Commodore Perry in the land of the shogun.* New York: Lothrop.

Boorstin, D. J. (1983). *The Discoverers: A history of man's search to know his world and himself.* New York: Random.

Bradbury, N. M., & Quinn, A. (1991). *Audiences and intentions: A book of arguments.* New York: Macmillan.

Capek, M. (1967). Change. In P. Edwards (Ed.), *The encyclopedia of philosophy* (Vol. 1, pp. 75–79). New York: Macmillan.

Carneiro, R. L. (1968). Cultural adaptation. In D. L. Sills, (Ed.), *International encyclopedia of the social sciences* (Vol. 3, pp. 551–554). New York: Macmillan & The Free Press.

Chirot, D. (1985). Social change. In A. Kuper and J. Kuper (Eds.), *The social science encyclopedia* (pp. 760–763). Boston: Routledge & Kegan Paul.

Coles, R. (1989). *The call of stories: Teaching and the moral imagination.* Boston: Houghton Mifflin.

Cross, D. W. (1982). Propaganda: How not to be bamboozled. In P. Eschholz, A. Rosa, & V. Clark (Eds.), *Language awareness* (pp. 70–81). New York: St. Martin's.

Downs, R. B. (1978). *Books that changed the world* (2nd ed). Chicago, IL: American Library Association.

Eschholz, P., Rosa, A., & Clark, V. (1982). *Language awareness* (3rd ed.). New York: St. Martin's.

Greenfeld, H. (1978). *Sumer is icumen in: Our ever-changing language.* New York: Crown.

Grolier multimedia encyclopedia (1994). Danbury, CT: Grolier.

Grun, B. (1991). *The timetables of history: A horizontal linkage of people and events.* New York: Simon & Schuster.

Hayakawa, S. I., & Hayakawa, A. R. (1990). *Language in thought and action* (5th ed.). Fort Worth, TX: Harcourt Brace Jovanovich.

Hyslop, J. H. (1910). Change. In J. Hastings (Ed.), *Encyclopaedia of religion and ethics* (Vol. 3, pp. 357–358). New York: Scribner's.

Kennedy, C. (1993). Teaching with writing: The state of the art. In *Language arts topics papers*. Williamsburg, VA: College of William and Mary, Center for Gifted Education.

Kniep, W. M. (1991). Appendix 3: Social studies within a global education. In W. C. Parker (Ed.), *Renewing the social studies curriculum* (pp. 119–123). Alexandria, VA: Association for Supervision and Curriculum Development. (Reprinted from *Social Education*, 1989, pp. 399–403.)

Leo, J. (1993, March 8). Spicing up the (ho-hum) truth. *U. S. News & World Report, 14* (9), 24.

National Aeronautics and Space Administration. (1988). *Earth system science: A program for global change.* Washington, D.C: NASA.

National Aeronautics and Space Administration (1990). *The earth observing system: A mission to planet earth.* Washington, DC: NASA.

Newmann, F. M., & Wehlage, G. G. (1993). Five standards of authentic instruction. *Educational Leadership, 50* (7), 8–12.

Perry, T. S. (1992a, October). E-mail at work. *IEEE Spectrum, 29* (10), 24–28.

Perry, T. S. (1992b, October). Forces for social change. *IEEE Spectrum, 29* (10), 30–32.

Petroski, H. (1992). *The evolution of useful things.* New York: Knopf.

Ravitch, D. (1990). *The American reader: Words that moved a nation.* New York: HarperCollins.

Rutherford, F. J., & Ahlgren, A. (1989). *Science for all Americans: Scientific literacy.* New York: American Association for the Advancement of Science.

Scarre, C. (Ed.) (1993). *Smithsonian timelines of the ancient world: A visual chronology from the origins of life to AD1500.* New York: Dorling.

Seiger-Ehrenberg, S. (1991). Concept development. In A. L. Costa (Ed.), *Developing minds* (Rev. ed., Vol. 1, pp. 290–294). Alexandria, VA: Association for Supervision and Curriculum Development.

Sher, B. T. (1993). *Guide to science concepts: Developing science curriculum for high ability learners K–8.* Williamsburg, VA: College of William and Mary, School of Education, Center for Gifted Education.

Singer, I. B. (1962). *Stories for children.* New York: Farrar, Straus, and Giroux.

Tamplin, R. (Ed.) (1991). *The arts: A history of expression in the 20th century.* New York: Free Press.

Thompson, M. C. (1991). *The magic lens: A spiral tour through the human ideas of grammar.* Unionville, NY: Trillium.

Vogt, E. Z. (1968). Culture Change. In D. L. Sills (Ed.), *International encyclopedia of the social sciences,* Vol. 3 (pp. 554–558). New York: Macmillan & The Free Press.

Yolen, J. (1992). *Letting Swift River go.* Boston: Little, Brown.

An overview of the outstanding titles available from the

CENTER FOR GIFTED EDUCATION

A PROBLEM-BASED LEARNING SYSTEM FROM THE CENTER FOR GIFTED EDUCATION FOR YOUR K-8 SCIENCE LEARNERS

The Center for Gifted Education has seven curriculum units containing different real-world situations that face today's society, plus a guide to using the curriculum. The units are geared towards different elementary levels, yet can be adapted for use in all levels of K-8.

The goal of each unit is to allow students to analyze several real-world problems, understand the concept of systems, and conduct scientific experiments. These units also allow students to explore various scientific topics and identify meaningful problems for investigation.

Through these units your students experience the work of real science in applying data-handling skills, analyzing information, evaluating results, and learning to communicate their understanding to others.

A LANGUAGE ARTS CURRICULUM FROM THE CENTER FOR GIFTED EDUCATION FOR YOUR GRADES 2-11

The Center for Gifted Education at the College of William and Mary has developed a series of language arts curriculum units for high-ability learners.

The goals of each unit are to develop students' skills in literature interpretation and analysis, persuasive writing, linguistic competency, and oral communication, as well as to strengthen students' reasoning skills and understanding of the concept of change.

The units engage students in exploring carefully selected, challenging works of literature from various times, cultures, and genres, and encourage students to reflect on the readings through writing and discussion.

The units also provide numerous opportunities for students to explore interdisciplinary connections to language arts and to conduct research around issues relevant to their own lives. A guide to using the curriculum is also available.